JOYFUL JOURNEY

An Adventure in Eldercare

Grace Sweatman

Onward!

GRACE SWEATMAN

EDITED BY JIM SWEATMAN

Tellwell Talent
www.tellwell.ca

ISBN
978-0-2288-1786-4 (Paperback)
978-0-2288-1787-1 (eBook)

Disclaimer

The content of this publication is based on actual events.
Names have been changed to protect individual privacy.

Table of Contents

Joyce Teiber, Robert McKeogh (Dad), and Grace Sweatman, July 1945.

Dedication

This book is dedicated to my five beautiful children, their spouses and their families. They have actively listened to the many stories I've shared with them throughout the years. They have accepted the fact that this book is not about them or their exploits, nor indeed their patience with my career engagement. They have only ever encouraged me in this adventure.

And to Catherine, my dear friend and colleague of so many years, a special note of thanks.

And to my youngest son Jim, who set up my blog, corrected my grammar, faithfully edited the stories and compiled them into a meaningful chronology.

And to my Dad, who gave me my love of storytelling.

Thanks to all of you. I love you.

Mom

Grace Sweatman and Heather Janes, 2019.

Foreword

Heather Janes, CEO of Christie Gardens

For as long as I can remember, my mom has been a storyteller. Whether it was to teach, inspire, or simply make us laugh — over dinner at home or in a team meeting at work — stories were a part of the fabric of life. Someone in the room would always say: "Grace, you have to write that book!" or "Another one for the book!"

Finally the book is here — a collection of stories and lessons that I know will inspire and uplift. Snapshots of a career in eldercare, shared by a leader who was never satisfied with the status quo and who led our team through a powerful culture change at Christie Gardens. It has been a blessing to learn from and grow my career under such an influential leader in the world of eldercare.

I'm so happy that these stories are being made available to a broader audience, and I know you'll enjoy them as much as I do.

Our journey continues at Christie Gardens. May these stories and lessons inspire your own journey.

Beginning a New Adventure

A Sign

Spring 1974

I t was a sunny but cool afternoon in Toronto. I was driving to my friend Ruth Pinkston's home for an afternoon visit. My youngest daughter, Heather, then 15 months old, was sleeping in the back in her car seat. The traffic was steady as I headed east on Bloor Street toward the entrance to the Don Valley Parkway en route to my destination. Bloor Street is four lines wide at this juncture. We would be crossing over the Bloor Viaduct with its wide sidewalks bordered by substantial concrete fences.

I stopped at a traffic light and was surprised to see a well-dressed elderly lady hurrying along the sidewalk ahead of me. *Where could she be going?* This was not an area frequented by pedestrians. As I pondered her presence, she turned toward the concrete railing and began to try to climb over. The ravine lay many metres below.

This could only become disaster. With no clear plan other than to stop her climb, I pulled to the curb, abandoned my car and sleeping daughter, and raced to her side.

"Be careful Ma'am, you could fall!"

She turned toward me with tears flowing and sobbed, "I'm trying to find my son. He was a pilot. He was shot down by the Red Baron. I know he's down there somewhere. Let me go. He needs me." Her grief was overwhelming her.

I was joined in my remonstrations by another gentleman who had also stopped. He said I should call the police, and he would take care of her. "There's a phone booth over there."

I have only a dim recollection of my frantic trip across the four lanes of traffic. Fortunately, I was able to connect with the telephone operator without using a coin. With trembling voice and scattered thoughts, I managed to ask for help. I could barely provide details of my location.

By now all traffic had stopped and a passing police vehicle had come to investigate. Help had arrived and would intervene. She would be safe.

Breathless and on very shaky legs, I returned to my car and my still-sleeping daughter. After several deep breaths and the return of strength, I proceeded to Ruth's house.

The lady's distress and confusion had been both insightful and very disturbing.

Poor soul. I knew the Red Baron was a famous German WWI fighter pilot who had shot down many enemy planes. *Could she have only imagined her son was one of them?* Whether or not he had been, she believed he had. He needed her and that was all that mattered. Her pain was very real.

"I just had a very sad experience, Ruth." I recounted the story, and with a moment of unintended foresight, I stated, "The lady was very distressed. She needed me at that moment, and I'm grateful I was there to intervene. I wonder if this was a sign that I'll work with seniors in the years ahead."

My Lady on Bloor Street still occasionally comes unbidden to my mind.

So many years later, there is still no simple cure for her kind of confusion and resulting pain. We can only reach out a hand with respect and loving concern to others who need us.

I am so grateful to have been given that privilege. It has indeed been a Joyful Journey.

Lesson Learned

Prophecy can be self-fulfilling.

The Sweatman Family, 1978.

But Until Then

My career in eldercare began in 1979.

For the previous 16 years I had enjoyed the awesome privilege of being a stay-at-home mom. My five children were now all thriving in full-time school.

I had begun considering a return to school to develop a skill I could employ in the workplace. My first consideration was Seneca College's

Library Science Certificate. *Could my practice of reading, often 2 books a week and occasionally more, be put to good use?*

In the midst of that consideration, and having made an appointment with Seneca College, my neighbour Yvonne had encouraged me to consider applying for an interesting part-time job. She was quite enthusiastic.

"I know you would be perfect for this job!"

I took Yvonne's advice and met with the administrator of Shepherd Lodge, a small home for the aged in Agincourt, owned and operated by the Pentecostal Benevolent Association of Ontario.

Reverend Lynn Pinkston was a friend and seemed pleased with my interest in the post.

During the interview, I absorbed the details of the job with excitement. This wcould be a new adventure, and one I felt I could embrace.

I considered the schedule and determined that I could make this commitment without fully disrupting home and church commitments. And so I accepted the post as a part-time evening receptionist, for three evenings a week.

The fact that I could begin to make a contribution to the income of our household was an especially gratifying consideration.

It was a dream job for me and a totally new set of experiences.

I would answer the phone, welcome guests, visit with residents, and respond to their inquiries or concerns.

During the ample free time remaining in my early evening shifts, I would sit at the grand piano in the front lounge with the group of residents who had gathered. We would chat about the issues of the day and reminisce about the past. Our time of often enlightening conversation would be followed by singing favourite hymns together — a very pleasant time indeed.

I quickly developed a keen interest in the "old-timers" who gathered around.

There were ladies and gentlemen who, at this stage of their lives, were at peace with their circumstances and waiting for their life journey to end. Some were feisty forces to be reckoned with, while others, even those struggling with challenging physical losses, maintained peaceful demeanours.

One very elderly gentleman, 98 years of age when I met him, saw his role as that of greeter at the front door. He would introduce himself to visiting strangers with a well-worn soliloquy: "Welcome to our home; my name is Mr. Jones. I do not drink, dance, smoke or chew, nor consort with those who do."

Nor would he be dissuaded from this self-appointed role. He was simply a familiar part of our community.

A very comfortable routine soon emerged in our evening visits. I would choose familiar hymns, known to this cohort, and after a few moments ask if there were any special requests. Mrs. Beckett, a

97-year-old lady who had lived in the home for several years, would always respond. She knew, unfailingly, exactly what she wanted us to sing: "What a Day That Will Be." The familiar old hymn looked forward to life ending and being with Jesus.

I knew and loved the old hymn, but also felt an impulse to remind them that there was a current chapter.

So each night that we sang together, I would follow the familiar request with another composition: "But Until Then, My Heart Will Go On Singing."

The lyrics beautifully expressed a vision for the future and at the same time our connection to the present.

That activity may not have swayed their thinking at all, but it reinforced a principle for me. My heart would go on singing, and with joy I would carry on.

I adopted the motto "Joyful Journey" as a life theme and the name of this book.

Lesson Learned

To this day I am reminded of both our privilege and our responsibility. It is indeed a Joyful Journey, and I am determined to carry on, until that day!

What Really Matters

S hepherd Lodge, my introduction to the world of eldercare, had been built in the 1950s as a not-for-profit, faith-based home for the aged, providing accommodation and services for 150 residents.

Located in Agincourt, a neighbourhood in Scarborough, Ontario, it was a "kind and gentle place" serving frail elderly persons, many of whom had spent their working lives as ministers and missionaries.

By 1979, when I began my new career, its physical plant had already become somewhat outmoded. The majority of residents shared their accommodation in semi-private or ward rooms with communal washrooms. Baths were provided once weekly with staff support.

Even those who were privileged to live in private rooms shared their washroom with a neighbour. In the entire home there was only one truly private room with its own washroom.

Into that special place came a retired missionary of renown. Mrs. Smith and her husband had journeyed in 1920 into Borneo. The last part of their lengthy journey, with all their possessions, required several days riding on ponies led by tribal porters. Theirs was an exciting history of lives spent serving people whose language and customs were far removed from their Canadian experience. We would hear and revel in stories of their experiences and exploits.

Their interludes on Canadian soil were filled with presentations and storytelling in their home churches. They were spoken of with respect and sought after as speakers.

Mrs. Smith had remained in missionary work following the death of her husband and was indeed a world traveller. When she finally retired in 1980 at 90 years of age, she chose our Home for her final years.

We were honoured to have been chosen to serve her and were quite pleased with our ability to provide her with our one special private room.

Mrs. Smith was six feet tall, carried herself with dignity, and had a sonorous voice and commanding presence. Over the months of her time with us, we had worked diligently to respond to her expectations.

She was well-experienced in providing direction and was quickly identified as a force to be reckoned with!

Oh, how we tried! And then we learned what really mattered!

One reminder of the outdated activities in seniors' homes at that time was the practice of using a public address system for communications between staff members. Messages would be relayed throughout the building and phone calls announced. This occurred frequently throughout the day.

At Shepherd Lodge this system was also used to broadcast the Sunday morning chapel church services and any other special event held in the lower level auditorium. The church services were for all to enjoy, including the staff on duty. After all, we were a faith-based home, and this was to be expected!

I was dismayed by the practice and felt that the frequent communication of messages via voices coming out of the ceiling was loud and confusing.

Broadcasting the church services throughout the building seemed to me to be an invasion of privacy. Not everyone should be held captive to the singing and preaching frequently emanating from the ceiling.

The actual broadcast controls were part of the audio system housed in the front office. The decision whether to broadcast, and then the responsibility to manage volume levels, was in the hands of the administrative staff.

The day came when Mrs. Smith was the announced special speaker at the monthly Wednesday afternoon Women's Missionary Council meeting. I discussed the meeting with Marjorie, our executive assistant, and together we decided we would not broadcast this ladies' meeting throughout the home. After all, it was for ladies only and might be best left to be heard only by those who actually attended.

The moment came when an important telephone call for the administrator was received in our office. Marjorie, intimidated somewhat by the mechanics of the system, forgot completely about the meeting in the auditorium and quickly activated the "on switch" in order to advise the administrator of his call.

At precisely that moment, our revered resident was speaking to her audience.

It was to become a never-to-be-forgotten moment. Before we had opportunity to realize Marjorie's error, Mrs. Smith's sonorous voice boomed from the overhead speakers.

"And then I came to Shepherd Lodge!"

And, with a pause for emphasis and renewed vigour, she drew out the words:

"ONE BATH A WEEK!"

We both lunged for the switch and were able to silence the system before we heard anything more. However, the message was received. No appreciation for the private room, nor our unfailing efforts to satisfy our important resident.

What really mattered to Mrs. Smith? The issue had already been addressed to the director of care following a forceful request, and the decision was made that we could not make an exception for one resident, no matter how important she was. She could only have "one bath a week!"

One might wonder if there had been divine intervention on Mrs. Smith's behalf.

Important decisions were made that day.

The practice of the overhead communications would cease. No more services broadcast throughout the home.

An investment would be made for an audio system that would be located in the auditorium and used solely for that purpose.

And most important, Mrs. Smith was offered two baths a week!

And we learned some important lessons.

Anything that could go wrong, likely would!

Just because we had always done it this way did not mean it had to continue.

Understanding what really mattered to our residents was important to their quality of life. I would return to this lesson throughout my career; indeed, it become one of the central lessons on my Joyful Journey: Policies were not to be tools in the hands of leaders but merely guidelines to be carefully considered. Perhaps there would be a way!

Lesson Learned

Some people want more than one bath a week! Take the time to learn what really matters. Don't let established policies get in the way of providing individual attention.

Certificate in Gerontology

A good friend called and told me about a new program of study offered by Open College and accredited by the Ryerson Polytechnic Institute. It would be available to mature students with some on site classes but the bulk of the study to be broadcast on CJRT-FM radio.

The area of study was called Gerontology. I had never heard the word before! A study of aging? Now that sounded interesting. And so, with some misgivings about my lack of knowledge but eager to learn, I signed up. I was indeed a mature student so previous schooling, or lack thereof, would not be a deterrent.

I was part of a small group, the first class in their new certificate program. The next three years were enriched by this delightful experience. I learned a new vocabulary, began to understand the importance of research, and was surprised that my opinions were not of interest but the publications of others must underlie any subject I addressed.

In the second year the classes were offered not only on the radio but also on campus, in the heart of downtown Toronto. Wednesday afternoons saw me take public transportation downtown to the Eaton Centre, enjoy a restaurant supper, and then head to class. It was a completely new adventure and I loved it. Me, a student, studying an exotic subject, and doing reasonably well in my studies.

In the final year I took a course on Environmental Design. The Professor, Pamela Hitchcock, was a specialist in Urban Planning and loved the subject. Her enthusiasm was contagious.

Our major assignment was to choose a downtown public building, assess it for accessibility and prepare a report for presentation to the class. It was the highlight of my year.

I chose the old bus terminal near Bay and Dundas downtown. My research was simple: visit, listen, observe, and critique. Today the subject of accessibility is at the forefront of societal expectations. Not so then!

I recall my surprise at what I experienced.

The handicapped phone booth was on the second floor, but there was no elevator. The men's washroom was two flights down a dark narrow staircase. The sound system was almost unintelligible. The seating could not have been more uncomfortable. The waiting room, such as it was, was open to the diesel fumes of idling buses.

And so I took pictures, developed a slide-show, and wrote a script. To add spice to my presentation I played a recording of a comedy routine I had heard on an old Bill Cosby record, as background noise. In a piece titled "A Nut in Every Car", Cosby imitates the announcements in the New York City bus terminal. His premise was that homeless men, heavily under the influence of alcohol, would be brought to the terminal to make the announcements. The resulting mimicry was hilarious.

My presentation was a hit with much laughter in the telling and listening.

After three years I graduated! It was a great experience. To my delight, I was presented with not only my Certificate in Gerontology, the first graduating class of six students, but also a special award for Environmental design.

I continue to pay tribute to the excellent professors who were patient and encouraging with this mature student. I would never be a scholar but I could find humour in almost any subject.

The icing on the cake occurred this year. My much loved professor of Environmental Design moved with her husband, also a professor in Urban Planning, into Christie Gardens. She insists that the award was for overall achievement, not just my comedy routine. I will choose to believe her!

Incidentally, the Toronto bus terminal has been renovated. I wonder if they ever heard of my presentation! The comedy routine is still out there somewhere. And I have an ingrained appreciation for the need for accessibility in all buildings.

Lesson Learned

Never stop learning.

Bleeding Hearts

After one year with increasing responsibility in administration, and additional hours dedicated to the activity programs, my role evolved further. The board of directors had approved a new post, Assistant to the Administrator, and I had been offered that opportunity. I eagerly embraced the full-time assignment.

The administrator, Reverend Lynn Pinkston, was close to retirement. Rev. Pinkston had no compunction about assigning responsibilities to me that may have been perceived to be beyond the understood scope of my role. I shared the same lack of compunction in accepting.

Every day was a fresh adventure.
My ignorance was bliss!

We did agree together, however, that if an educational opportunity came my way, I should enrol. My credibility in leadership needed that boost. And who knows? I might actually learn something.

And come my way it did.

The association serving not-for-profit providers of care and services, then known as the Ontario Association of Homes for the Aged and today known as AdvantAge Ontario, had collaborated with the Ontario Ministry of Health and developed a one-week intensive training program for new administrators. They were eager for participants and accepted my application, even though I was not officially in an administrator's role.

Within a few moments of the start of the program, I realized that I was in a potentially embarrassing situation. My classmates, seven new administrators, had many years of education and experience behind them. They engaged in active conversation, competing it seemed to prove their knowledge. They understood *per diems, occupancy,* or in their language, *bed days.* They had faced inspections and fire safety reviews, knew the rules in food-handling practices, and had dealt with labour code and human rights issues. And on it went. And I, a newbie with a dream simply to *do good* serving seniors, was about to be exposed.

And then I realized it did not matter.

My purpose was not to compete with my classmates but to learn. I probably would fare better overall because I had fewer pre-conceived notions. It would not be a pass or fail experience.

I actively engaged in the full week of mind-numbing information; presentations, which caused anxiety; and assignments, which revealed my weakness. I was definitely on information overload.

The last afternoon could not come quickly enough.

In the final moments of our week, two gentlemen, one a retired fire inspector and now a Ministry of Health consultant, and the other a retired administrator with many years of experience, left us with their words of wisdom.

From the Consultant:

"You will face inspectors who will give directions with which you may not agree. Do not assume their edict is the final word. Own the situation. You have already responded to inspections and been diligent in your actions in response. Learn all you can about the rules and stand your ground. It's called 'risk management' and you will practice it every day. Your success in this arena will depend on your 'risk management practices' being well-informed, not feelings-driven."

And from the Retired Administrator:

"You will be faced with difficult decisions in your role. There will seem to be conflicting priorities. You will need to balance kindness and doing good with resources and accountability for the use of those resources. If you learn nothing else, learn this: never let your bleeding heart rule your bloody head!"

And so I returned to my role as assistant to the administrator, not only wiser in the understanding of how much there was to learn and the challenges I might face, but also emboldened to "Do Good and Do it Well."

Lesson Learned

Do Good and Do it Well. Even this early in my Journey, I already knew that it was not enough to simply desire to do good, or even to serve well. I had to learn how to work within the system in order to manage both.

Binders

Fresh from my intensive educational experience, my desire to "do good" was immediately put to the test.

The board of directors of Shepherd Lodge had accepted the sales pitch of a management company that their services would assure an improved quality of care for our residents. Their message was compelling to the board. It said that: we needed policies and procedures; we needed oversight by professional representatives in the sector; we could save money with their approach; we would all benefit; and there would be no downside.

The decision to hire their services soon leaked. The grapevine worked overtime.

Who would be in charge? What changes would be made? Would any staff lose their jobs? Who were these people anyway? Might we lose our faith-based identity with these managers?

For a time, even I got caught up in a swirl of negative gossip and conjecture.

The silence from the existing hierarchy made the matter more challenging. A learned principle emerged: *If there is no information provided, someone will fill in the gaps and provide their own.* And provide it we did.

It was not a happy time. The day came and the new consulting team arrived. Their first action was to clear space on the shelves in the front office and install an ominous-looking bundle of binders. These were our new policies and procedures. We were to study them and apply the principles in a timely fashion. They would answer anything we needed to know!

I determined quickly that I had a choice to make.

Fight the new direction, continuing to use joy-sapping stress energy, or model a different standard, welcome the newcomers, and embrace their directives. I chose the latter and decided I would try to make it work.

The administrator would be retiring in a few months. He needed the transition to be as smooth as possible.

I would be the good girl, the voice of reason.

Those binders, however, flummoxed me. I quickly learned a principle that continued with me throughout my career. Policies and procedures were important, and for consistency and the safety of residents and the reputation of the organization, should be followed.

However, no binders or, later in my journey, legislation could guarantee quality care for our residents.

That could only come from the heart of skilled staff members.

The only binders that will be effective must be developed by the people actually practicing the principles, not merely placed on shelves as the solution to every problem.

The management company did, over time, make an important contribution to the maturing of the organization. However, the binders, touted as the magic cure for every ailment, became dust collectors.

Many years later I met the original nursing consultant from the management company.

She greeted me warmly and we reminisced together. She revealed how nervous she had been with the new contract and the leadership expected of her. She remembered the binders and agreed they were props to appear important.

She also comforted me with her recollection of the strained atmosphere, and expressed her appreciation of my positive support in an otherwise negative situation. She expressed regret that I soon accepted an employment opportunity elsewhere and didn't enjoy the benefits of her involvement.

I learned several valuable principles

When trouble is brewing, be part of the solution. *Do not add to the problem.*

The board of directors were the legal owners of the home. They had the authority to make important decisions regarding its operation. *Embrace the decision or move on.*

It's amazing how much damage can be done by one negative voice. *Be the exception to the rule.*

Or as I used to sing with my children:

**"You've got to
accentuate the positive,
eliminate the negative,
latch on to the affirmative and
don't mess with Mr. In-Between."**

Lesson Learned

Don't waste your time on binders you did not develop on your own! Developing binders is a healthy process, especially for an established organization that wishes to codify their best practices — but policies alone are horrible teaching tools. The binders and policies are guidelines and best practices, not a strict set of rules to be followed at the expense of individual attention and care

Another Step in the Adventure

May 1982

The previous year had presented a steep learning curve. Every day was a new challenge. The administrator, my supervisor and friend, was preparing for retirement. He gave me, his newly appointed assistant, free rein to tackle the everyday situations that would have historically been his responsibility. I was eager and learned quickly.

The Key Challenges as I Saw Them:

Fill the House. Occupancy statistics were less than satisfactory. We needed to carefully review the admission criteria, which often turned away applicants.

Develop a better relationship with the nurses. This group was convinced they were overworked and not respected. They resisted admitting residents who had care needs that would add to their workload.

Oversee the dining services. The open kitchen design echoed the unconstrained noise of meal prep and service, with little consideration of dining comfort.

And the Outcomes as I Saw Them:

Within the year, the House was filled.

We were actively reviewing the admission process.

If consistently monitored, the kitchen was quieter.

There were many other opportunities for personal growth. I was unconstrained by knowledge that comes from experience and was bolstered by some successes.

Eventually, my boss settled on his retirement date.

Who would lead upon his departure? Not likely me, as I knew enough to know I didn't have the experience to be a legitimate candidate.

The executive director who oversaw the home as part of his portfolio was a distant threat. He didn't know me, nor me him. However, I was comfortable in the knowledge of my successful endeavours and saw no need to worry.

And then came the day of reckoning.

The administrator, my friend, retired. The appropriate recognition had been extended and expressions of appreciation abounded.

The next morning, the executive director, now in charge until a successor was named, called me into the library across the hall from my office. What followed was the great awakening!

Who authorized my decision making?

Why had I confronted nurses?

Yes, the House was full, but the care levels were heavier and the nurses stressed.

Who gave me the authority to make the admission decisions?

And on it went. A deflating and distressing experience.

My heartfelt efforts appeared to be for naught. I had been faintly aware that my eagerness and decision making did not please everyone.

There had been complaints that I did not know my place.

And now the reality of the impact of the murmurings was hitting home. It was very apparent I did not have his favour. The future would be very different.

I returned to my office very discouraged and close to tears. My prayer was simple: "Lord, I will not be able to work for this man. Help me, please."

As I entered the door the phone was ringing. The receptionist told me that a Mr. Alexander wished to speak to me. I hadn't heard his name before and was somewhat reluctant to take the call. I would rather have retreated and had a good cry!

However, wisdom prevailed.

"Good day, Mrs. Sweatman. My name is David Alexander. I am the chair of the board of an organization that is building a not-for-profit seniors' residence on Yonge Street in the heart of Rosedale. Your name has been recommended to me as a potential candidate for the leading role, that of administrator. I would like to meet with you and discuss this opportunity."

And the next step in the adventure began.

Shepherd Lodge ultimately chose an excellent candidate to replace my now-retired friend. I had an excellent opportunity to launch my career, and I left my post satisfied that I'd made a meaningful contribution.

Lesson Learned

Leave well. Everyone knows the expression, "Don't burn your bridges," yet time and again I've seen colleagues "burn bridges," often while standing on them!

Mr. David Alexander and Grace Sweatman, 1982.

Eleventh Floor Test

June 1982

The slender, dapper gentleman made his way carefully across the construction rubble to greet me. He was dressed in a pale blue seersucker suit, with white patent leather shoes, and a white construction helmet. His smile was disarming and warm. He seemed very pleased to meet with me. The rubble was the site of the sixteen-storey seniors' community under construction in the heart of the city.

My first sensation was consternation.

Why on earth had I agreed to this interview? What little introductory information I had was somewhat daunting. I had no experience in marketing to seniors nor in operating a high rise seniors' community. I knew nothing about leases. I had never been in a role requiring me to select and lead staff. My only experience with seniors was my adventure at Shepherd Lodge.

I had experienced a three-year learning curve that I could never have anticipated and was now meeting Mr. Alexander at his request for an interview for the role of administrator of this new project.

"Let's make our way to the office we have just set up. We will take the stairs, as the workmen need the elevator, and it is an open construction elevator."

And so we began our climb. As we reached the fifth floor, I was starting to feel winded and a not a little weak-kneed. I heard his voice in the back of my head. He had told me we would go to the new office.

What had not registered until now was that he told me it was located on the eleventh floor.

With absolute certainty I knew that this was the test of my candidacy, and that I could never make the eleven-floor climb.

It seemed of no concern to Mr. Alexander. He stopped briefly on the fifth floor to talk to two dust-covered workmen. Their conversation gave me a very brief respite. I took a deep breath and soldiered on! *Never did an unfinished rudimentary office look so attractive.*

First test passed!

For the next three hours, Mr. Alexander shared his vision for this new community, to be called "Fellowship Towers". The residence would provide extensive services including full meal service and excellent support services for the 300 seniors who would choose it as their home.

It was a not-for-profit venture, a new model that could inspire others.

He felt very strongly that a carefully selected leadership team, operating with faith, integrity, and respect for the seniors, would enhance the final years of those who chose it as their home. He was convinced there was a better way than the options currently available for his elderly friends.

He was a high risk entrepreneur, a visionary, and a gracious gentleman. His vision was contagious. Our conversation was lively.

I began to see an opportunity I could never have anticipated.

And then, the moment of truth! Mr. Alexander asked a life-changing question: "Mrs. Sweatman, would you be prepared to throw your hat in the ring, market this project and become its future administrator? I will continue in my role as project manager, see it fully built and prepared for occupancy, and continue as president and chair of the board of directors."

My uncertain response seemed to cause him some surprise. "Is there anyone else's hat in the ring?" I asked.

"No, absolutely not. I am offering you this job. You would need to start in six weeks. Take some time to think about it and get back to me."

"I don't need any time to consider. I would love this job and would be honoured to work with you."

It was indeed a defining moment in my career and life. For the next thirty-three years, I worked with this gentleman, in this role and roles of increasing responsibility elsewhere.

I had passed the eleventh floor test and soldiered on.

Looking back on it now, it's clear that climbing those steps to the eleventh floor was a key part of the Joyful Journey, but at the time, the climb itself was anything but joyful.

***

Lesson Learned

There would be many eleventh-floor experiences in my future. The fifth floor would be merely a brief respite. The challenge would be to remember there would indeed be an eleventh floor, no matter what it looked like on the fifth!

Fellowship Towers

Marketing

Fellowship Towers was a new model in its day.

Located in the heart of the city with Rosedale subway station within one block; a short stroll to fine shopping on Bloor Street; ease of access to theatre and art; small but well appointed suites; expansive amenity space; a commitment to fine dining; well-groomed, respectful, well trained staff (well, they would be!); flexible services — all at a fair price!

I marketed our accommodations
and services with pleasure.

I was convinced we would be a highly desirable option for many city-dwelling seniors. Our occupancy commitments were over 75 per cent, with two more months before we opened.

Into that picture, requesting a tour, came a very elderly matron, her companion by her side, her chauffeur waiting at the curb.

Mrs. Brown was a forceful personality. She was prepared to contest every statement I attempted to make. Her challenges were not unexpected. They were, however, made more challenging as Mrs. Brown was profoundly deaf. She wore older hearing aids with cords from each ear to the amplifiers in pockets in her blouse. However, no matter how I tried and in spite of the amplifiers, I could not make myself heard to her satisfaction. So I began using a writing pad to assist in our discussions.

For over two hours I would write, extolling a feature. She would verbally challenge me, and I would write a response. We had an effective communication system working.

Our dialogue was very extensive. Some might say exhaustive.

Her companion said not a word, just looked anxious.

On the tenth floor, when Mrs. Brown had begun expressing interest in a double suite, with underground parking for her chauffeur and accommodation for her companion, I began to become concerned. What if she actually chose our home. Could we ever meet her expectations?

Mrs. Brown looked out the full-length window in the double suite she was considering. The building backed onto the beautiful Rosedale Ravine. It also overlooked the open cut of the subway. At that moment she observed a subway train making its way south to the Bloor Street Station.

With an expressive frown, my guest stepped back and inquired: "Won't that be noisy?"

I must have been overtired from my marketing efforts. Whatever the reason, good judgment fled. I stepped toward her and with both of my hands tweaked the cords extending from her hearing aids, and then laughed heartily.

My response did not need the writing pad. My guest was only briefly startled, and then she took my hands and laughed with me. It was time for a hug!

We ended the exploration on that note and returned to the lobby. She left Fellowship Towers smiling, her companion smiling beside her, apparently having also enjoyed the encounter. Her chauffeur greeted her at the door.

Her parting words?

"Thank you, dear lady. Great tour. Nice, but not for me!"

Wise matron and relieved marketer!

Lesson Learned

Not every inquiry is a good candidate for the services you offer. I would encounter this lesson frequently over the years. I learned that applying a thoughtful and empathetic "filter" to prospective community members increased our likelihood of being able to serve them well.

Opening Day!

We had worked long and hard to see the opening day of Fellowship Towers. Rentals of the 300 suites had reached the 75 per cent mark. Inquiries and visits continued at an active pace.

The construction process had been long and complex. Our project manager, Mr. Alexander, had been unrelenting in his insistence on quality work by each tradesman.

Mr. Alexander had not had a day off in eight months.

Marketing of the suites had been very vigorous. Mr. Alexander, with his mellifluous voice, had performed the radio advertising program for this new community, and had become quite well known on the CFRB radio airwaves. I had conducted countless tours and signed residential contracts with the seniors and their families.

The new staff team had been hired and introduced to their assignments. The first grocery order was in place. Furniture and bedding had been installed in each suite. At 10:00 p.m., the night before opening, we gathered together in the new lounge and joined hands as Mr. Alexander led us in prayer.

The first weekend promised a move-in of 80 residents.

There was a palpable excitement in the air on that beautiful Friday autumn morning. The excitement was heightened by the arrival of the first moving trucks. But we hadn't realized we should have scheduled their arrivals, *so it was first-come, first-served*!

Within two hours we had trucks lined up as far back as Bloor Street, a two block stretch. And then the real adventure began!

Before we were able to give access to the first truck in line, a large cement truck and a City of Toronto maintenance truck with a work crew and foreman arrived outside the front door.

They had come to repair the uneven sidewalk that had been reported to them some six weeks earlier. Mr. Alexander had clearly communicated his concern on behalf of the soon-to-be residents. He was convinced there would be falls caused by the trip points, and this needed to be corrected.

There was no dissuading this crew, who began immediately to jackhammer out the old sidewalk and prepare for the new. Amid much discussion, occasional shouting, and gesticulating, the decision was made by the truck drivers and Mr. Alexander that the move-in processes could begin using wooden ramps from each truck across the newly laid sidewalk to the front door.

And so began a very long day.

Each piece of furniture had to be carried down the ramps while anxious seniors waited. There were only two elevators. The front lobby reflected ongoing chaos. Nerves were getting frayed. Our commitment to *gracious service no matter the circumstances* was being sorely tested.

And then came relief.

The new concrete had been poured and the work crew were smoothing the surfaces of the half-block repair. Suddenly, and from who-knows-where, a large and very beautiful golden retriever began the trek from one end of the sidewalk repair to the other. Each time he lifted a paw he disturbed the freshly poured concrete and left fresh paw prints. Slap, lift, splash, and repeat. He made his way for the half block leaving an artistic trail of fresh concrete behind him.

Who will ever understand the dynamic that ensued?

Truck drivers waiting to deliver their furniture loads, work crew under pressure to get the job completed, and seniors and staff watching from the lobby broke out into laughter that quickly became uproarious.

The dog seemed remarkably unperturbed. Perhaps he was the "angel unawares."

Whoever he was and wherever he came from, the outcome was a remarkable relief of tension and a reminder that the universe would continue to unfold, no matter our plans and schemes.

I've often wondered if there were actual paw prints left behind. One thing was certain: the highlight of the day, our friendly visiting golden retriever, more than eclipsed the stressful drama for the seniors moving in, the truck drivers discharging their loads, the work crews charged to see the job completed, and the long-suffering team who had worked toward this day for many months.

And thus began the life of this unique residence, serving seniors in the heart of the busy metropolis.

Lesson Learned

Humour can save the day.

Mr. William Wilkie, 1974.

An Emerging Opportunity

September 1982

Fellowship Towers had been open one week. The busyness exceeded our expectations. It was a very satisfying experience. The new residents were still moving in, several each day. Housekeeping had begun their weekly service for each resident. The meal service was improving as the new staff team developed routines and an understanding of individual resident's wishes. The myriad of demands for group living were being addressed.

We were creative and flexible and succeeding.

And then, on the first Friday after our exciting opening day, a team of three gentlemen arrived and asked if they could use my offce for a meeting. Of course they could. Mr. Alexander, Mr. Wilkie, his friend and colleague, and a third gentleman unknown to me came to the offce together.

Mr. Wilkie and Mr. Alexander had now been instrumental in developing two residences.

The first, in 1974, was New Horizons Tower at the corner of Bloor and Dufferin. A high rise seniors' residence, it was sponsored by Dovercourt Baptist Church and was part of the planned relocation of their church. Their current older place of worship had been no longer adequate to serve the young, growing congregation. To stay in the core of the city, as was their commitment, required an infusion of capital. The residence with the church included in the building was the result of their initiative. A very complex and unique project.

The second, in 1982, Fellowship Towers on Yonge Street, was our newly opened residence. This project had been built on the success of New Horizons Tower with a new, more modern and highly-desirable design. And now the key players were planning again.

I was working nearby while they used my office, so I could hear their conversation. The key speaker was Mr. Wilkie.

"We need to look to the future. When our residents develop increasing health needs, our capacity to serve them well in this setting, or in New Horizons Tower, is in question. With the current scenario, we have to counsel seeking a nursing home elsewhere, the very situation we were trying to avoid when we began this work. We want to be certain that the values and life principles of our residents are respected and that our promise to provide for them to the end of their lives is fulfilled."

Mr. Wilkie continued, "I propose we seek a location nearby for a nursing home that could serve residents from these communities. I will provide a personal interest free loan of $100,000 to begin to cover developmental costs. Our friend here is a broker who can assist us with acquiring land and licenses. He is willing to forego the usual fee deposits for us to get started. Mr. Alexander still has the energy and can project manage once again."

The whole idea should have been very exciting. I was the first to learn of their plans. Instead of excitement, I felt frustration and anxiety.

When two of the gentlemen had said their goodbyes and only Mr. Alexander remained, I confronted him with my concern. "We have barely begun Fellowship Towers and have a mountain of work ahead of us. How can you be getting into something else when you are needed here? Can't you at least wait?"

Mr. Alexander heard me out and then kindly informed me not to worry. "I chose you because I believed you could handle the complex challenges that would emerge. You are doing very well. I have full confidence you can continue. The future of our residents is at stake here. We must not fail them."

Here was another time on my Journey when I learned that the overall mission was the key driver as we looked to the future. Stopping to rest was not an option while the mission was unfulfilled.

And that was that!

The success of Fellowship Towers would require five years of unrelenting determination and effort to see it on a healthy course. During that time, the gentlemen would acquire land and funding, purchase nursing home licenses, and develop a unique community where you could be "Home for the Rest of your Life" and part of "A Community You Can Have Faith in."

Christie Gardens opened in August 1984.

And that is another story!

Lesson Learned

Never rest on your laurels; always look to the future.

Here Kitty

The night-time security guard was seriously concerned. One of our "little ladies," Miss Clark, was regularly making her way in her night clothes, late in the evening, from her suite on the 4th floor.

She would be carrying a dish and a small bottle of milk and would come down the back stairs, use a rear door to exit, and make her way carefully to the parking lot of the Canadian Tire store next door.

He would hear the swish of the door closing and hurry out to check. He had tried to discourage her from coming down late at night, especially dressed in her night clothes. Her indignant response brooked no further interference.

"Kitty is thirsty. She needs this milk."

"I don't see any kitty. It's not safe out here at night."

"She comes later when we're gone. I'll pick up the dish in the morning."

He shared his concern with Mr. Alexander, who visited regularly.

It was a time when the technique of "reality orientation" was being touted as the best solution for folk experiencing memory loss and disorientation. Reality orientation had its roots in caring for mentally disturbed veterans returning from war, many of whom would have been suffering from what we now know as post-traumatic stress disorder (PTSD), or what they called "shell shock" at the time. The thought was to provide information to the distressed person in order to re-orient them to their current surroundings. This reorientation was hoped to improve their sense of place and time, and increase their feelings of safety and security.

Mr. Alexander, however, may not have heard of this technique. Nor would he likely have subscribed to it if he had.

We discussed our concerns together and he advised me not to worry. He would talk to her.

On his next visit he sought her out. "Miss Clark, you do not need to worry about kitty anymore. The Sweatman boys who work here as security guards were sorry for the kitty. They wanted a pet, so they took her home with them. Kitty is safe now. You will not need to go out at night to give her milk anymore."

Miss Clark heard him out and then thanked him for his help. She would talk to the boys and let them know how to take care of her.

Problem solved! We could relax. She wouldn't be going out at night anymore.

Mr. Alexander then thoughtfully went one step further. He sought out the "boys who had taken kitty home" so that they could be prepared if our little lady approached them. The conversation was a little disconcerting, but they promised to support his story if she did.

Bases covered. So much for Reality Orientation.

Our sense of peace lasted one week.

Miss Clark approached Mr. Alexander with apparent glee. "Thanks for trying to help. Please tell the boys, however, that Kitty missed me and she came back!"

Miss Clark lived at Fellowship Towers for three more years. A family member, finding that no amount of counsel or redirection would work, bought Miss Clark a very realistic toy kitten. Kitty became her constant companion and accompanied Miss Clark to the dining room for all her meals. She had a reserved seat and her own cushion upon which to be comfortable. Her friends were very patient with her and did not attempt to dissuade her. Dining room staff gave special permission for this accommodation.

No more trips out at night. A contented
"little lady" and a reminder that strength
of character can transcend reality.

Somehow, in her sweet disposition and with her ability to solve her problem, she taught us a lesson in kindly, flexible responses to the people we loved and served, no matter their disorientation from reality.

Lesson Learned

Another reminder that understanding and empathy are key to individual service. I am certain that there are binders full of policies that ban pets from the dining room. In our world, any such policy would be put to one side for the imaginary pet of a resident.

David Alexander, 1981.

Smooth Sailing and Clear Skies

1983

Fellowship Towers was quickly established as a desirable option for seniors, providing high quality accommodation and services, in the heart of the city. I had been privileged to be its leader through marketing, staffing, setting policies and operating principles, and welcoming its first residents.

There was only good news with Fellowship Towers.

We were enjoying 100 per cent occupancy and the beginning of a waiting list. We'd been successful in recruiting experienced nurses and dining staff. My assistant was performing well and showed promise for future leadership. The atmosphere was upbeat, the attitudes kind and encouraging. An excellent sense of community had developed.

Mr. Alexander was very proud of Fellowship Towers, into which he had poured heart and soul.

Never comfortable at rest with a need unfulfilled, Mr. Alexander decided that the time had come for him to move on to the next vital chapter. So in 1983 he accepted the role of chair of the board of the newly incorporated Christie Gardens.

I was invited to join the fledgling board of the new endeavour. The board experience was an invaluable part of my Journey.

Under Mr. Alexander's leadership, we saw the project through from design to construction and opening. It was a daunting experience.

Christie Gardens opened in October 1984. As a board member, I was aware of some struggles, but mercifully not required to solve them. This is not to say that Fellowship Towers was all smooth sailing and a fait accompli, but compared to what we were hearing about Christie Gardens, we felt quite pleased with ourselves.

One would have thought it was time to relax a little and enjoy the fruit of my labour at Fellowship Towers. However, that was not to be. I had an eye on Christie Gardens as a board member, but also as a potential step on my Journey.

Lesson Learned

Perhaps I, like Mr. Alexander,
was not comfortable to rest with a need unfulfilled.

Moving On

Christie Gardens was in its third year. Occupancy was high, but the atmosphere reflected considerable discontent. The nursing home appeared to be a very challenging environment. Our board meetings focused entirely on the large printouts of the financial status, with little awareness of the people who were being served.

I felt a stirring of concern for its future. I also felt frustration at issues that I believed were not being addressed.

Mr. Alexander, as he had done for me at Fellowship Towers, gave counsel and encouragement in his oversight but was doing his best to allow the current administrator freedom to lead. And then the administrator advised Mr. Alexander that he had decided to move on to another opportunity. He felt it was time for a new leader. He gave six weeks' notice.

Mr. Alexander called the same day to offer me the post.

I hesitated only briefly. I would be leaving what presented as a success in my ongoing career. I would be leaving hand-picked staff and a group of seniors whom I knew and loved.

On the other hand, I saw the opportunity to lead Christie Gardens into its envisioned future as a continuing-care community.

My heart left the comfortable and embraced the challenge. Throughout my Joyful Journey, I had never taken the easy path. Indeed, I saw this as another challenge. I accepted with pleasure and committed myself to a one-month notice period at Fellowship Towers

For the Journey to continue, it was time to step out of my comfort zone and embrace this new adventure.

Lesson Learned

Be careful what you wish for. You might just get it.

Christie Gardens

Sign the Documents, Please

Years before I joined Christie Gardens, I was a member of their board of directors. What follows is part of their Joyful Journey.

Christie Gardens was now in the last phase of construction. The project was the result of months of planning and negotiations between the "volunteers extraordinaire," Mr. David Alexander, and Mr. William Wilkie, Ministry of Health officials, lending organizations, and others who typically come to the table when a new development is underway. The eight-member board of directors of this new not-for-profit venture had also been recruited.

The original dream had been to build a nursing home.

This home could be available now on a priority basis to seniors from either of their two successfully established residences in the heart of Toronto — Fellowship Towers and New Horizons Tower. The new nursing home would fulfil the commitment to continuing-care for folk needing these services. Funding for care would be provided by the Ontario Ministry of Health.

When the financial analysis was undertaken, however, it quickly became apparent that the original plan for a stand-alone nursing home was not viable. Another factor in the decision making process was the emerging awareness that single rooms — the original model for seniors' accommodation — were no longer a desirable option. More private space, better amenities, a closer semblance of "normal" living was in demand.

And so the concept of a continuing-care-community was developed, from independent living through to a full-care nursing home.

The resulting plans were unique. Apartments, a retirement home, and a nursing home, all in one place and housed in a seven-storey building. "The Last and Best Move You Will Ever Make" became a familiar marketing slogan.

With the approval of the Ministry of Health, 88 licenses were purchased from the owner of two long-outdated nursing homes. Mortgage approval was granted by Canada Mortgage and Housing. The new exciting venture was being advertised on CFRB Radio.

A critical juncture in the completion of the project had been reached. The newly constructed nursing home was ready to welcome its residents. The retirement home and apartments were 90 per cent completed. An administrator had been hired, a gentleman with many years of experience in nursing homes. The leadership team had been expanded with critical posts filled. Busses and ambulances for the transfer of residents had been chartered. A caterer had begun to set up the kitchen.

The only remaining obstacle to welcoming the nursing home residents and their staff was for the Ministry of Health Director to sign the operating agreement.

Tension was running high. Residents and staff were eager to move into their new home. The board of directors were aware of the need for the services to begin, with the resulting much-anticipated revenue. But the Ministry of Health director had not yet signed the essential documents, with no reason given other than process impediments. In the fourth week of full readiness and no apparent timeline for approval, Mr. Alexander, project manager and chair of the board, decided this delay could no longer be afforded or tolerated.

Mr. Alexander telephoned the Ministry of Health director's office and advised the receptionist that he and the administrator of the new nursing home would be coming to Ministry offices that day. He expected the approval documents would be signed. He then packed his small overnight bag, and with his concerned colleague accompanying him, headed for downtown.

"David, why do you have an overnight bag? What are you planning?"

"I am not leaving that office without the signature on the documents. If the director won't see us, I will tell them I will be staying all night if necessary."

"David, you cannot threaten the Ministry."

"Harm is occurring, both for the seniors and our financial stability. He must sign."

The duo arrived mid-day as planned. They were advised by office staff that the director was busy and could not see them.

"We will wait." And so the sit-in began.

Others came and went. Office staff members requested that the gentlemen seek a formal appointment.

"We will wait. Thank you."

Late in the afternoon, there was a flurry of anxious activity. The director departed quickly with several staff members accompanying him, avoiding any contact with the gentlemen waiting in the office.

Once they had departed, the remaining staff member advised them that the director and his assistants had left for the day for a dinner obligation, so they would need to make an appointment for another day.

Mr. Alexander's response: "You were advised that I would not be leaving until the documents were signed. I have not changed my mind on this. I would recommend you contact your director and advise him accordingly. I have my overnight bag with me."

With much consternation, the staff member "left holding the bag" contacted the director's assistants and relayed the message. Several anxious calls ensued and finally the message they needed to hear was delivered.

"The director is requesting you leave and return in the morning. He's making a personal commitment that the documents for approval to open the nursing home to residents will be signed and ready for you to pick up. Please leave now so we can close the office."

Mission accomplished.

Mr. Alexander, and his by now exhausted administrator, left the office and went home, returning early the next morning to pick up the freshly signed documents.

Within a few days, the chartered busses, and in some cases transfer ambulances, arrived with new residents.

Families and friends assisted in setting up their rooms. The accompanying staff members were received and their duties assigned. And the new adventure began.

Since that fateful day there have been many diverse chapters at Christie Gardens. It remains, however, a standard in negotiations when all else fails:

Lesson Learned

Gracious, unrelenting determination for a well-considered cause can win the day! Especially if you believe it will!

E. Coli Outbreak

June 1987

It was late in the day, a beautiful summer day in June 1987. I had begun my new assignment ten days earlier with much anticipation and excitement. I was going to be in charge of Christie Gardens, with its apartments, retirement home, and nursing home — an all-in-one community in the heart of central Toronto.

I'd been on the board of this not-for-profit organization since its inception three years earlier and had been eagerly waiting for the day I could "run it."

The beginnings at Christie Gardens had been challenging and frequently very difficult — financial challenges, staffing challenges, and resident challenges.

Finances were woefully inadequate, with no corporation to provide support.

Continuing employment of the existing staff of the two nursing homes from whom we purchased our licenses was promised in the purchase agreement. However, no selection process was in place, simply a promise to continue employment. Unions were in place and fiercely protecting incumbent staff members regardless of their suitability or the quality of their performance.

Residents, 88 of them, were either seniors discharged from mental health institutions; indigent, previously homeless seniors; or younger people who required an institutional home due to disability.

Christie Gardens had opened with a vision to operate as a community where no matter what changing needs the seniors might face, it could continue to be their home.

This commitment was clear and received well by seniors who chose to move into the apartments or retirement home. There would be no need to move to another location in the most critical stage of life.

The chair of the board, Mr. Alexander, was very gifted and focused on operating a warm and welcoming place. His Christian values were expressed in the mission statement: "In response to God's call, we are committed to serving with excellence those who have chosen Christie Gardens as their home."

And now he had asked me to take responsibility for the day to day operation of the home. The board of directors had approved this decision, and the future was bright for me — and hopefully for them and Christie Gardens, and most of all for the seniors we would serve, now and into the future.

We had ambition, "to be the best in town." We had heart, evidenced by our decision to provide financial support to residents if needed. We had good business skills on the board, but no experience in the challenges of running a nursing home funded by the Ministry of Health, nor in serving this resident family with its complex needs.

Back to my bright afternoon in June! The phone rang and the receptionist told me it was someone from Sunnybrook Hospital calling. A very serious lady on the line advised me that a resident from Christie Gardens had tested positive for E-Coli 0157. This was a very contagious intestinal disease and she would be reporting us to Public Health and the Ministry of Health.

Toronto Public Health would no doubt be arriving to begin their investigation!

E-coli! The only thing I knew about this communicable condition was that 23 residents had died in 1985 at a large nursing home in London, Ontario as a result of an outbreak.

And so began a series of lessons for life!

Over the following 16 days, we were visited daily by all levels of health agencies: municipal, provincial, and federal. Each agency had their own agenda, and it didn't take long to realize that we did not share the same agenda.

They inquired about the condition of the resident, who most fortunately was recovering, and then about the condition of the kitchen. This was another matter. The cause of the infection could well have been poor food handling practices. The caterer, faced with this serious stress and ongoing scrutiny, was apparently unable to rally to affect a clean, well-ordered kitchen.

The officials digressed into how we handled our incontinence products, as fecal matter was a potential agent in the transmission of this infection. The city representative didn't want another incinerator operating and spreading noxious fumes, the outcome if we burned our disposables, nor did they want their landfill plugged up by the same products.

If we used reusable products there was no assurance we wouldn't transmit the infection to others, as the reusable products were laundered by an outside agency.

They had no solutions, only aggressively expressed concerns.

The real crux of the matter for them, however, was the recommendation, communicated with increasing urgency, that we should (must) provide a news release revealing the incident and our responses.

At this juncture, self-preservation kicked in! Perhaps it would be better stated, "Christie-preservation."

No, I would not release an announcement of our situation.

No, no one would report us to the media. That was not our world.

No, I would not release an announcement and risk becoming a memory for the future of a home that had this experience.

I actually wrote the news release in the event that it might be needed. But for sixteen days, we did the "news release dance."

The situation did resolve itself. The resident, although she had suffered considerably, survived the infection.

The news release did not go out. I measured the risk daily and owned the decision not to issue it. Christie has been vindicated many times over by well earned good news in the media.

A new caterer was sought and contract provided without the usual formal budget or tendering process.

Desperate times called for desperate measures.

The relationship with Sodexo, the caterer chosen by me because they were purported to be eager for business and therefore flexible, continues to this day with a proven history of successfully overcoming a very difficult challenge. And our investment in the dining services, the most engaging part of each resident's day, has made it one of our notable services, with regular commendation by residents, friends, industry peers, and academics.

There were several lessons learned during this crisis.

You get what you pay for.

The budget for the caterer provided by the Ministry was not adequate for the provision of a satisfying dining experience. When the decisions that were made about meals at Christie Gardens were based solely on funds available, the outcome was predictably very poor.

The agenda of government service agencies is not necessarily the same as yours!

Their acknowledged concern was that the public would be assured they were doing their job in response to the outbreak. Any potential impact on the reputation of our community was of no concern to them.

Just because someone told me to release the information publicly did not mean I was obliged to do so.

Make your own decisions based on what is best for you and your organization, not on what others believe to be best. In the end, the risk and the outcome will be owned by you.

Good faith is earned.

Although it was evident we were struggling in the operation of our community, we treated our residents, their families, and our staff with kindly respect. There was "goodwill in the bank," an invaluable commodity. Never underestimate the importance of maintaining non-confrontational relationships in a quarrelsome world.

In a critical struggle, the leader is on her own!

I recall the sense of abandonment, with the Christie Gardens advisory physician out of town on vacation, our board relieved I was taking care of this, and a nursing director who was new and unequal to the challenge.

The show was all mine!

This too shall pass.

And indeed it did. And we were older and wiser, with a new caterer, a commitment to enhance the dining experience, and transparency where it mattered: with those we served and those serving.

Lesson Learned

This too shall pass. I was fortunate that I encountered this challenge several years into my Joyful Journey. I might not have had the experience or fortitude needed to come through unscathed if this had happened during my first job!

23 Pages of Non-Compliance

August 1987

T he E-Coli outbreak and the hiring of a new catering service were freshly behind us. We continued to make progress in improving the quality of life for those we were serving.

Mealtimes, especially in the apartment dining room, were a more satisfying experience, and staff sensed somehow that working conditions were improving overall.

As the new leader, I was determined to build relationships with the staff members. They would soon realize that we were honest, well-meaning, and generous. There was one staffing issue that I had to deal with right away, and that was the termination of the nursing director.

It was clear from the outset that she was not happy in the position, and one afternoon we sat down together and came to an amicable agreement regarding her departure. We agreed that it would be best for her to leave that same day, feeling that it would avoid discomfort for all parties.

I was excited about the prospect of building a new team, replicating the atmosphere I had cultivated at Fellowship Towers.

Moments later, while I was making notes about future plans, there was a knock on my door — my now-former nursing director informed me that there was a Ministry of Health inspector at the front desk. There had been a complaint and they were here to conduct an investigation.

Nursing inspector! This would be a completely new experience. I had no idea of the requirements under the Nursing Homes Act, nor the inspection process and potential outcomes.

I invited the inspector into my office.

She advised me that a family member had complained that we were understaffed. An interesting complaint overall, as I knew of no staffing regulations we could have violated. I responded that I was new to the position and had been concerned about the care in the home and had indeed just dismissed the nursing director a few moments before.

So bring it on … whatever "it" was.

Three hours later, the inspector came back to me, well into the evening by now, and handed me a sheaf of papers. I was being served a 23-page report on the areas of non-compliance with Ministry of Health regulations.

In light of the fact that I was indeed concerned about the care of the residents and had taken definitive action to address this concern, she would not request a formal Ministry of Health intervention but would give me time to report back to her on the actions taken to resolve the areas of failure.

That report became a benchmark for identifying the concerns that I instinctively felt but did not have the experience or knowledge to identify and address effectively.

For the next three weeks, with the help of a friend who was a nursing director in a large private nursing home in the city, we addressed the findings and made the necessary changes.

This became my crash course in operating a Ministry of Health funded nursing home. The actions taken to address the issues gave us a satisfactory report from the inspector on her follow-up visit.

I then presented two key recommendations to the board of directors.

The nursing home could not function successfully on the Ministry funding as it was.

Would the board consider allowing the surpluses from the remainder of the community to subsidize the operation? Yes, indeed they would.

Would they also approve an increase in the staffing to address the original complaint? Yes, indeed they would.

Timing is everything.

I knew that a difficult decision had to be made and followed through on.

Just in time! Trust your instincts. Others trust you. It's important you do not fail them.

Sometimes what seems the most grievous can be a blessing in disguise.

The complaint and the resulting inspection gave me the tools needed to get the job done. The nursing home would continue to be a challenge to operate, but the day to day care of the residents, our most important commitment, improved dramatically.

The incident was a defining moment for me personally and for the future of care in our home. Hindsight makes clear that it was a significant step in the Joyful Journey.

Several lessons came out of this experience, two worth noting here.

Never be afraid to acknowledge challenges and the need for help.

To have wasted time and energy while protecting my pride or reputation would have been seriously counterproductive.

I didn't know how the system worked nor what the requirements were under the Nursing Homes Act. I did know that I could be excused on this first round.

Taking definitive action was the most effective tool to inspire confidence in those around me. And those to whom I was accountable.

Not everyone with authority is an enemy.

The inspector had cause and authority to take drastic steps to correct the operating issues in the nursing home.

We were not deliberately creating an unsafe environment for our residents, but in fact the many areas of non-compliance gave serious cause for her concern. Our inspector chose to give us the opportunity to correct our shortcomings.

During her follow-up visit, she commended us and encouraged us to "seek excellence." Our expression of appreciation for her support set the course for the future of the relationship between Christie Gardens and the Ministry of Health.

Lesson Learned

Sometimes what seems the most grievous can be a blessing in disguise. Faced with criticism from outside, we might have taken a defensive posture, but instead we embraced the feedback and turned the challenge into a highly constructive exercise.

Art Deco Mantel Clock, by Friedrich Mauthe.

The Clock

1987

I had been in my post at Christie Gardens for only a few months. I knew very little about the politics involved in Ministry of Health funding mechanisms. In fact, I knew very little overall. Just a curious mind and a desire to care for seniors.

As a member of a not-for-profit-association representing owners and operators of seniors' homes, I was invited to serve on an eight-member committee. The committee would be led by a government representative and would be comprised of other government officials, an economist, and nursing home operators.

Our assignment was to make recommendations regarding a new proposed funding model for long-term care, a very complex and potentially contentious issue.

It was a "heady" experience, with several meetings and conference calls.

I had considerable difficulty not revealing my lack of knowledge while attempting to make a meaningful contribution to the discussions. The remainder of the committee members seem well-informed.

The final meeting was a conference call. We had submitted our recommendations on the new funding model some weeks earlier and were eagerly awaiting the final report from the government representative on our committee. He would advise us of the decisions that had been made by the Ministry of Health officials and the Treasury Department.

I cannot speak for my team members, but I was stunned by the final financial proposal.

I could see no correlation between our carefully constructed recommendations and the proposal that was subsequently adopted. *Where had I lost track or misunderstood?* There was little response from the remaining team members. Perhaps they understood better the subject matter and the norm of the consultative process.

The call ended with expressions of appreciation and promises to get together again one day. We were then bade farewell, with one exception. The leader asked the economist to stay on the line. There were some matters he wanted to discuss.

I made a quick decision. I would not hang up but would stay on the line and listen to their conversation.

I rationalized that it was a reasonable, albeit sneaky, plan. After all, I had earned the right to understand what had actually occurred.

The committee members each hung up with the audible beep that occurred on disconnect. I sat silently and listened. It became apparent that the gentlemen's conversation was neither confidential nor of any import to me. I also belatedly realized, with dismay, that when I disconnected, the same beep would sound, giving away my presence.

Oh dear, what to do. I decided I had better wait it out and disconnect only when they ended their conversation.

And then, fate intervened!

The beautiful antique Art Deco mantel clock gracing my credenza, recently repaired and marking time with melodious Westminster Cathedral chimes at each quarter hour, began its solemn duty.

The resulting cacophony of sound could definitely be heard by the gentlemen on the call. Rather than staying on to "face the music," I hung up and immediately burst into gales of laughter. The incident became one of my stories that I so delight in telling.

Lesson Learned

"Be sure your sins will find you out."

Ontario Long Term Care Association

The Adventure on
the Dark Side

"Join the Ontario Nursing Home Association," my mentor and chair of my board advised me.

"But Mr. Alexander, that's the 'dark side.' They exist only to make a profit on the care of the elderly."

"They are not evil! They are good business people who have chosen to be in this essential business. You will learn a great deal from them."

And so, with some temerity, I attended a regular meeting of the members of the ONHA (now the Ontario Long-Term Care Association, or OLTCA). I was welcome as a guest but would not be eligible to vote. It was a very exhilarating experience — excellent content, a well conducted meeting, with many diverse voices engaged in the dialogue.

They covered a myriad of subjects, some I had never before heard mentioned. The room was filled with owners, operators, administrators, and leadership staff. It was quickly apparent they were not evil! Perhaps a slightly stronger focus on government funding than I had experienced in the association for my fellow not-for profit providers, but serving the same populations with the same care needs.

And so Christie Gardens joined the Ontario Nursing Home Association.

For the first few years of my membership, my participation in ONHA was limited to these monthly meetings. I began to see familiar faces and to understand better the language of the business.

I grasped more clearly the nuances of the proven inadequacy of Ministry of Health funding, frequently-changing legislation, the inspection processes and their impact, and the politics of advocacy.

We were operating in a contentious and challenging political environment. When a new government was elected to power, the association was faced with building relationships with a new field of politicians, and preparing for the next round of funding decisions and operational changes.

Further, media exposés sometimes resulted in new laws, which some in political power believed would result in improved quality of care for those they served.

It was during those fascinating days that I developed a personal view, expressed whenever I could find a forum.

"You cannot successfully legislate quality of care for those we serve. The only hope for quality lies within the heart of the leaders overseeing the service."

The organization and its care for the people will be the lengthened shadow of its leaders.

The degree of impact that the OLTCA leaders could have on government policy was complicated by a second party, the association serving the not-for-profit providers. The two membership groups, frequently at odds in their approach to advocacy with the Ministry of Health.

It seemed to me each group was weakened by their divergent tactics. I especially respected the solution-oriented posture of my chosen association.

Although my view was never publicly confirmed, I became convinced that the Ministry of Health officials had learned how to manage the two associations, often leveraging one against the other in negotiations. What a waste of energy!

Could I play a role in the leadership of OLTCA?

Could I be elected to the board of directors? And why would I want to do so?

I identified four key personal factors in making my decision.

My learning opportunities would be enhanced. I would be strengthening my performance in leadership at Christie Gardens.

I believed strongly there should be one voice to government. I would strive to be an influence in promoting the collaboration and co-operation of the two associations.

My sense of mission was heightened. Here would be an opportunity to influence my colleagues in their care of the elderly. Could we all operate kind and gentle places?

I loved to lead! This engagement would certainly fuel that drive.

And so, with heart in hand, I began the journey. The outcomes were very satisfying. I would look back several years later and assess the impact of my decisions.

My business education was dramatically enriched through my engagement.

We were still two associations, but the not-for-profit membership in OLTCA had multiplied five-fold, a much stronger voice of influence.

There were moments I felt naive in my dream to see heart-led change in the overall purpose for being. Not just a return on the investment, but also the increasing focus on resident-centred care. Not just saying it, but doing it! More and more, however, this vision was coming to fruition. There was no question I was at a "table of influence."

Over a period of seven years I was privileged to participate actively in OLTCA. I served on committees for two years. I was elected as a director representing the then-small group of not-for-profit members. This two-year term was followed by another two-year adventure as VP of Government Relations.

To my great satisfaction and indeed delight, I was elected president of the association in 2008. I did indeed love to lead!

**I made highly valued friends and connections,
many of them continuing to this day.**

And then Christie Gardens startled the world of associations and providers of long-term care by selling its licenses and becoming a fully self-funded care home.

And that is another story!

Lesson Learned

You want to lead? Go for it!

Threatened

February 2008

My tenure as vice president of government relations for the Ontario Long Term Care Association (OLTCA) included meetings and discussions with government officials and, hopefully, the Minister of Health. Our relationship at that time with the Minister had become acrimonious. OLTCA advocacy for increased funding resulted in hostile responses, especially as media exposés fueled his disdain.

For two years the association had sought an appointment with the Minister to present our carefully researched and executed brief on the need for additional funding. He had finally agreed to meet with us.

And so the "brave soldiers," a team of three representing the OLTCA: our president, our vice president of government relations — the role I filled, and our CEO, with our brief in hand, headed to Queen's Park.

Although my colleagues had been to this office before, for me it was a new experience. We hurried through the halls of power and presented ourselves to the Office of the Minister of Health. We were welcomed by his assistant and asked to wait in his office. He was in the "House" and would be along shortly.

The room in which we were seated was well appointed, but the most dramatic impact was the photo gallery surrounding us of former Ministers of Health, and the dates of their tenure. The atmosphere warranted whispered conversation while we waited.

And then after a forty-minute wait, the side door opened and our Minister strode into the office followed by two young advisors. He was visibly very angry. Unknown to us, he had just been aggressively attacked by the opposition party.

In the days preceding our visit, the leaders of a large union representing hundreds of our employees had made a public spectacle of the Minister. They performed a demonstration on the front steps of Queens Park, revealing what they expostulated was the practice of the owners and operators of long-term care. Using incontinence briefs as props, they poured water through until the brief could hold no more. With loudspeakers and media in place, they delivered their message:

"Your failure to adequately support our workers, Minister, means the residents are not changed until the brief is full."

This assault on the Minister was ugly and poorly informed. We had not been apprised of their intentions. The Minister took it as a personal humiliation.

When we became aware of the incident, we felt our best posture was silence. The resulting media uproar might achieve our goal of increased funding, but the union performance embarrassed all of us, especially the residents we served.

And then two days later our Minister was challenged again in the House, while we waited to present our case for increased funding. The timing could not have been worse.

Without the usual introductions, he aimed his fury at us.

"How dare you come to see me? I have just been humiliated in the House as a result of the union demonstrations. Where were you when this was happening? Where was your voice of support for the efforts I have made on your behalf? You're coming to ask for more money. Fat chance of that happening!"

"And who are you?" he shouted in my direction. I responded with a shaking voice and attempted to explain my role in OLTCA and introduce the home I served.

"Christie Gardens, that's not-for-profit. What are you doing here with these people?"

There was no opportunity for response. He then directed his next shouted salvo at my colleagues.

"Don't ever expect support from me! I'll fix you! I will propose legislation that will require the signature of the unions in our next operating agreement. They'll have a say in the directives governing your homes."

I recall today as if I was still in that room. The implications of his threat were ominous.

He took a breath from his rant and I managed to speak up. Instead of advocating for my fellow operators and their association, I returned his salvo.

"Oh no you won't! Christie Gardens will leave the system first!"

That was our last word!

We were unceremoniously ordered to leave and to take our brief with us.

Our little band of three was breathless. It was some time before we could collect our thoughts and discuss "What next?"

We certainly had not succeeded in our mission. If anything, the relationship between the Minister and OLTCA had now deteriorated further.

Did the minister follow through on his threat? No, he did not. And we did subsequently deliver our brief to his officials.

Did Christie Gardens follow through on my threat? Yes, one of the wisest moves we ever made!

Could I have read our future? It was two years before Christie Gardens announced its intention to sell our licenses and leave the system. It would seem, however, the die had been cast!

The universe does unfold. Sometimes in mysterious ways!

Lesson Learned

Another self-fulfilling prophecy, or perhaps, the heart knew what the mind had not yet realized.

Meanwhile, Back at Christie Gardens

My Medal!

A practice I believed in and dictated to others in my role as the CEO was to have all outgoing mail approved by me and all incoming mail opened and reviewed by me. I actually enjoyed the work involved, but most important to me, I stay tuned in to all aspects of the operation. Some might say it was an exercise in control. So be it! I believed it gave me effective oversight of the activities of the house.

With the outgoing mail I could be certain that the written communications on Christie Gardens letterhead not only were appropriate to the matter being addressed, but also maintained the standards of gracious non-confrontational responses, no matter the subject matter.

The system worked well until my absence of a few days caused a backlog of mail.

**Such was the case in the spring of 1992 upon
my return from a two-week vacation.**

My assistant cautioned me that the mail had accumulated and that I should focus on this task first. She had sorted the mail for my review without actually opening any of the letters. Advertising materials were put to side for later or to be simply discarded … my decision.

I dedicated my first hour to the task, noting that the advertising pile included something from Parliament Hill, no doubt political promotion of some sort. I put this pile to one side, expecting to discard most of it.

The day was full and the review of the mail wasn't completed but left for my follow-up attention the next morning. I debated simply discarding what appeared to be political advertising but on brief reflection thought I had better have a look.

**The creamy embossed paper was a clue
this might be something more.**

Indeed it was. To my complete surprise, I was advised that I had been nominated and selected to receive a medal struck to commemorate the 125th anniversary of confederation. Officially, it was the 125th Anniversary of the Confederation of Canada Medal, awarded to "Canadians who have made a significant contribution to their fellow citizens, to their community or to Canada."

An event to present the medals was one week hence.

The deadline to RSVP my acceptance of the honour and attendance at the event was the day I was reading the letter!

I could bring two guests only. I immediately responded in writing using the enclosed RSVP card and requested that my assistant follow up to be certain my response was received in time.

I confess knowing almost nothing about medals and the related protocol, but I could grasp the honour that was being extended. One week later, my chairman and our director of resident services accompanied me to receive the medal.

I'll never forget the ceremony and illustrious recipients. Next to me in the line of honourees was Frank Shuster! Johnny Wayne and Frank Shuster were comedy superstars during my childhood, and I was slightly star-struck. The presenters were the Lieutenant Governor of Ontario, Hugh Jackman, and the federal Member of Parliament, the Minister of Foreign Affairs, the Honourable Barbara McDougall.

At no time, however, did I learn the identity of the person who had made the nomination.

There is, however, another story.

The medal is framed in a shadow box mounted on my bedroom wall. I consider it a treasure. It still gives me a thrill of personal pleasure each time I read the commendation.

There was little likelihood I would ever actually wear the medal, so I decided to order the half size replica and seek the services of a skilled framer to create a shadow box for the medal and signed certificate.

Magna Frame was a well known framing service and art store in Yorkdale Mall. I had frequently noted the quality of their work, including the framing of medals from military service displayed in their window. I left the medal in their capable hands with a promise from them of a two to three week pick up date. They would call me.

On week four, I followed up and was assured it would be ready soon. Another two weeks and the call finally came. My medal and certificate had been framed and were waiting for me.

The end result was excellent. I expressed my delight and grateful appreciation of their fine work. At that moment, the owner of the business stepped closer to me.

"Now that we have successfully framed your medal and certificate, we can confess the cause of the delay.

Our technician laid out the materials in preparation for framing and, reaching too quickly, spilled a full cup of coffee over the signed certificate. You cannot imagine our horror. After our frantic and ineffective efforts to clean up and dry the certificate, we realized we would need help.

The personnel in the Ottawa office responsible for medals and records responded well. Although there was some delay, they were able to create a new, freshly signed document and send it to us. The font on your name is slightly different. We actually think it looks better. There will be no charge for this service. We apologize for the delay. We are simply so relieved the problem was solved successfully. Congratulations on this honour."

Little did they know that this event would become an integral part of my Joyful Journey recollections.

The store did not stay in business, but I did.

Thank you to the unknown, kind person who took the initiative. And mercifully, my review of the two weeks of mail was just in time for my grateful RSVP.

Going forward, in any extended absence, my assistant was authorized to take the extra step of opening and reading incoming mail as it arrived. Any item of particular note could then be handled in a timely fashion.

Lesson Learned

Control has its limits!

Mystery in the Nursing Home

1993

It was early morning in the nursing home, and the director of care was very irritated. She confronted Ann, the housekeeper on duty that morning. "Why did the housekeeping department remove the window drapes in Room 101?" They were needed for privacy. She had received a complaint from the daughter.

Ann was very clear. She did not touch the drapes. She would never do that without telling someone. She promised, however, to look for them. Perhaps someone else had taken them for cleaning.

A Mystery to be Solved

Meanwhile, Catherine, the VP of Operations, was making her morning rounds throughout the nursing home when she was approached by a long-term resident. Mrs. Jones loved to sew and occupied her days with various projects. She would approach Catherine, thread in hand and sewing needles inserted in her apron, and ask that she thread her needles for the day. Catherine would patiently oblige, a pleasant ritual between friends.

There was something different today, however.

Mrs. Jones had made herself a new skirt. The fabric was a little heavy for the purpose, and the design of the skirt was certainly not haute couture, but it sufficed. Mrs. Jones was very proud of her new creation and, on Catherine's inquiry, swirled to show it off.

In that quiet moment, with the final needle threaded, Catherine recalled the conversation she had just overheard.

Mystery solved.

The drapes had been repurposed by Mrs. Jones. But how did she ever get them down?

When asked, she shrugged her shoulders and told Catherine that someone had given them to her.

Lesson Learned

Not every mystery will be solved.

David Alexander and Grace Sweatman, 1994.

10th Anniversary of Christie Gardens

October 1994

It was time to celebrate.

C hristie Gardens had opened its doors to serve seniors ten years earlier. Our founder, the president of our not-for-profit corporation and chair of our board, Mr. David Alexander, was committed to never losing sight of our history.

So celebrate we must.

Mr. Alexander also felt strongly that it was important we include well known public persons in our events, so we planned a Sunday afternoon gathering in our auditorium for residents, their families, and friends of Christie Gardens. Mr. Alexander would host our event and welcome everyone. We would enjoy a slide presentation of our ten year history. Our special guest would be recognized and bring greetings. We would then make our way to our spacious dining room for afternoon tea!

Ten years before, The Honourable Pauline Mills McGibbon had participated in our opening.

She was now fully retired and living close by. A legendary figure in modern Canadian history, Mrs. McGibbon was described as "Ontario's Eve" for all of her "first woman" accomplishments and accolades. First woman to serve as Lieutenant Governor. First woman to serve as a vice regal representative in Canadian history. First woman to lead the Canadian Conference of the Arts. First woman to head up the National Arts Council. Director of IBM, Imasco, and Mercedez-Benz, Chancellor of the University of Toronto and University of Guelph, etc.

Mr. Alexander felt he could convince Mrs. McGibbon to be our special guest and extended the invitation to her. She was most gracious, remembered Christie Gardens, and would be pleased to participate.

The next phase of Mr. Alexander's planning was to determine the protocols to be practised in welcoming, accompanying, introducing, and thanking our guest.

He worked out detailed instructions for each step of Mrs. McGibbon's visit.

Who, and how, we would greet her, make a brief visit to the office, accompany her to the auditorium, assist her to her seat on the platform, introduce her to the guests in the auditorium, enjoy our carefully planned program, and then make our way to afternoon tea once our auditorium event concluded.

Lest there be any doubt, Mr. Alexander wrote a script of all the steps to be undertaken. We were committed to his and our success in this endeavour.

We were committed to avoiding embarrassment at all costs.

One key item on the agenda, as an expression of our respect and appreciation for her visit, was the presentation of a bouquet of roses. I was given this important task. When, where to stand, and how to present. And, oh yes, the quality of the bouquet!

And so came the very special day.

We had ordered the bouquet of roses. In order to assure they would be fresh, we had located a florist who would be open on Sunday. We picked them up at noon as scheduled and delivered them to the

Activities office near the auditorium. They were indeed beautiful, 18 peach-coloured roses in a presentation bouquet.

While we waited for our guest, Mr. Alexander once again reviewed our respective duties. The exciting moment was finally here. Mrs. McGibbon arrived. She was very gracious, putting us all at ease. We followed our instructions to the letter and were feeling quite good about our performance.

And then a "snag"!

Just as the platform party was making its way from the elevator to the auditorium, Colleen, the team member assigned the task of delivering the bouquet to me at the appropriate moment, rushed to my side and in an excited whisper asked a critical question.

"Where is the bouquet? You told me it was in the Activities office, but it's not there."

"Look again, Colleen. We definitely left it there."

'Don't you worry, I'll find it or solve it somehow. Leave it with me."

There was no choice but to do just that.

And so the program proceeded. I don't recall much of what transpired. My mind was filled with thoughts of that bouquet. Where could it possibility be, and what would she do if she couldn't find it? What would I say if there was indeed no bouquet?

Mr. Alexander would never forgive us!

The time passed both slowly and quickly!

At the exact moment when Mr. Alexander was ready to introduce me to express our appreciation, there was a flurry of activity in the rear of the auditorium. The doors opened and there was Colleen, carrying the beautiful bouquet of roses. She ran down the aisle with a large smile and passed me the bouquet. "Tell you later!" she whispered.

The remainder of the afternoon passed in a blur of activity. Mrs. McGibbon left and our guests dispersed.

"Great memories, thanks."

"Beautiful event, and so smooth."

"So glad I was here."

We had celebrated, honoured residents, hosted our special guest, and satisfied our chairman with our response to his carefully crafted directives.

And now for the rest of the story.

One of our weekend receptionists, Patricia, a young university student, daughter of our director of dining services, Jolanta, was finishing her shift shortly before the planned arrival of our guest of honour.

She said goodbye to her mother as she was leaving. Jolanta had just finished with the dining room decor. "There are some flowers left over if you want them. They're in the office downstairs." Shortly thereafter, Patricia arrived back in the lobby with the "leftover flowers." She spoke to her replacement, now on duty at the desk.

"Aren't they beautiful? I feel like a bride." She pirouetted in the lobby and then left to drive the 45 minutes back home to Mississauga with her treasure.

When the frantic search for the bouquet began, the receptionist nervously recounted the experience to Colleen.

With much excitement, Colleen located Jolanta for her home phone number, and called Jolanta's husband at home. I have no doubt of the tone of that call.

"As soon as she gets home, she must come back with that bouquet!"

Patricia arrived home thirty-five minutes later to see her dad sitting on the doorstep.

"Back, back, you must go back. They need the flowers for their guest," he shouted to the startled young lady. No time for further discussion.

Patricia later recounted the horror she felt as she climbed back into her car and with frantic haste headed back to work. She cried most of the way, convinced her mother would never forgive her and that she would lose her job.

She pulled up into the driveway to meet Colleen just as Mrs. McGibbon ended her remarks and Mr. Alexander stood to introduce me. Colleen told us she does not recall how she got down to the auditorium. Staff members were lined up waving her on. She took a deep breath, opened the auditorium door, and, fulfilling her duty, delivered the much- travelled bouquet to me to present to our guest.

The wave of applause, especially from those in the rear who had become aware of the drama, must have seemed a little more than expected. However, it was a moment worthy of applause.

Our afternoon concluded without further incident.

Patricia did not lose her job. Colleen was our hero. Mr. Alexander was very pleased with our performance, and a never-to-be-forgotten 10th anniversary story was added to our history.

It never loses the humour in the retelling.

Lesson Learned

A reminder that anything that can go wrong, just might.

Just Waiting

October 1995

I met the visitor in the front lobby. She turned from the reception desk toward me.

"Are you the lady in charge?"

"Yes, that's me. How may I help you?"

"Can you tell me how my friend, Jessie, is doing? She was asleep when I visited her room just now."

I took her phone number and said I'd get back to her.

I asked the question of my director of care. "Please tell me about our resident, Jessie. A friend of hers wondered how she was doing, and I promised I would ask and let her know."

"Jessie has no major health issues other than frailty. The nurses are concerned about her well-being, however, as she seems somewhat depressed. They've requested a psychiatric assessment."

"How old is Jessie and how long has she lived at Christie Gardens?"

"She's 97 and has lived with us for five years. She lived in an apartment upstairs for three years prior to relocating to The Courtyard. She made the request to move downstairs when she began finding it difficult to manage her daily activities. Jessie is well-loved and a pleasure to serve. She seems to have withdrawn, however, hence their concern."

"And what will you do if this depression is the diagnosis, following the psychiatric assessment?"

"We could consider trying an antidepressant"

"For a 97-year-old? I would hope you don't go that route! By all means, request an assessment, but please, keep me informed of the outcome."

And so I made a note of our discussion and waited for the report. Meanwhile, I did call her friend and provide assurance that Jessie was comfortable, with no serious health concerns.

The psychiatric team, a new service provided by the Ministry of Health, came to assess Jessie. I was anxious as we waited.

There had been considerable discussion in the public forum about the overuse of medications, especially as a means to manage difficult behaviours.

My knowledge was based on experience rather than education, yet I held to my belief that there had to be a better way.

The psychiatric team report was presented to me, albeit somewhat reluctantly, by the director of care. She was uncomfortably aware of my view on the use of anti-depressants for the frail elderly, and now especially for Jessie.

The report, however, was a well written account of the visit of the three team members and their time with Jessie. It gave excellent insight into her history and current status. The conclusion caused me a sense of relief and feeling of joy at the same time.

"We enjoyed our visit with Jessie. We spent considerable time in conversation about her life experience, her values, and how she felt now. The team agreed together that no intervention was needed. Jessie made it quite clear she was not depressed. She's had a long, full life. She's now simply waiting for Jesus to come and take her home."

**I was instantly reminded of an old hymn:
"Oh, Lord Jesus, How Long, How Long?"**

Jessie was another defining moment in my journey into understanding and influencing the process of decision making in the care of our most vulnerable residents, especially as it related to mood or behaviour-altering medications. It was often a challenging exercise, requiring an unrelenting determination to find "a better way" to respond to their needs without undermining the practices of our health professionals.

Lesson Learned

Taking the time to understand the individual,
provided the best solution possible.

The Uninvited Dinner Guest

September 1996

O ur board of directors met bi-monthly. The seven members of the board would join me for dinner in a private dining alcove, then convene in my office for their formal meeting. Our time together enjoying a meal was important. It was a time for building relationships and getting to know each other better.

One such dinner was proceeding very smoothly. A director was sharing his story about assisting in a local homeless shelter. Mid-sentence, he looked across the table at me, and without changing the expression on his face or the inflection in his voice, said,

"Grace, there is a mouse climbing down the drape behind your head."

A mouse! He had to be kidding! No, he assured me he was not. Definitely a phobia of mine! *Feet up. Eyes closed.* What else could I do?

Our chairman, always ready with a solution, turned to me and suggested I get help from Catherine, our vice president of operations. Catherine could, and would, attempt to solve any challenge that came her way. I reflexively took his suggestion and, with some relief, hurried away from the dinner table.

A few steps into my journey to find Catherine, I realized this was a futile effort. What could she do that I could not? It wouldn't be fair to dump this problem on her.

And so, with no solutions to offer, I returned to the dining table.

Meanwhile, Mr. Alexander had taken matters into his own hands. He was holding the mouth of a tea cup against the wall beside him. He advised me that he had cornered the mouse behind the cup and was prepared to hold it there until all the residents had finished their dinner and left the dining room. And so we passed an awkward half hour waiting for residents to leave. Stilted conversation, some, mostly me, very uncomfortable while Mr. Alexander patiently held the cup against the wall.

When he was certain no residents would observe, he removed the cup and, to his surprise and disappointment, no mouse underneath!

I believe we all knew, deep down, that no self respecting mouse would allow himself to be corralled in that fashion.

We adjourned to the office for our meeting, aware our little interloper was loose somewhere. And if he was loose, there was no doubt he had friends.

The next morning, Catherine tackled the problem. She convened a diverse group of staff members and shared my story. They named themselves the "Mouse Squad" and developed an aggressive plan to make Christie a mouse-free environment.

In the next three weeks they eradicated 39 mice. However, we had not yet been able to find either the entrance points or the nests. And so, once more, Catherine came to the rescue. Her Mouse Squad had conducted inspections of all storage areas and public spaces, with a special focus on the main floor and lower level.

"We are going to inspect again."

Catherine and her housekeeping supervisor, Maria, began a systematic search once again.

"What about the chute room?" Each floor of the building had its own garbage chute, located near the elevator in a small room. Garbage deposited there fell to the lower level of the building.

"I'm sure they checked."

"We will check again."

On first glance there was no sign of nests or inhabitants.

"What's the skid over there used for?"

"Oh that's where our evening janitor stores the bird seed for the feeders in the courtyard garden. He's out of supply at the moment. He usually brings the feeders down here in the evening to fill them."

With a dawning sense that they had located the source of our unwanted visitors, Catherine and Maria walked over and carefully lifted the skid to peer underneath.

Not a nest, but a colony, including newborns.

Mice scattered in every direction. Some fled up the pant legs of the two ladies. Suffice to say, the ladies also scattered.

The story became part of hilarious memories at staff gatherings. The bird feeding saga was ended. The unwelcome tenants were evicted from the chute room.

The eradication aggressively continued with daily reviews until there were no more sightings nor evidence of their presence at Christie Gardens.

And the cup in the dining room?

Mr. Alexander gave it to the dining services manager, Michael, with the message it would need careful washing, as it had touched a mouse. Michael in his nervousness misunderstood the message. He became somewhat agitated and rushed into the kitchen crying out,

"Someone is trying to make trouble for us. The chair of the board found a dead mouse in his cup!"

"Mice" was an agenda item for the next board meeting. It became an item for hilarious memories of this group also.

In the serious business of caring for over 400 residents, there had to be room for comic relief.

I am not convinced that Mr. Alexander, who had finished his meal holding a cup against the wall, was quite as amused.

However, gracious gentleman that he was, he never spoiled our fun.

And the universe continued to unfold, with just a few less mice in it!

Lesson Learned

If you see one mouse, rest assured there are more.

5 Star Service

T he Intercontinental Hotel was known for its exceptional service. It was beautifully maintained. The staff team presented very professionally, and the dining service was second to none. What better place to inspire our operating directors to aim for top quality service at Christie Gardens?

I courageously called our workshop "Five Star Service in a Five Star Place."

I arranged for a two night stay, use of a meeting room, and several catered meals. The location was kept confidential until the day before we were to gather. Inspired they were.

We revelled in the gracious responses to our requests. We enjoyed sumptuous meals. Our rooms were well appointed. The linens alone were worthy of a return visit, if we could have afforded it.

And so for two days we worked at identifying how such a service standard could be achieved for our residents.

We could not provide the furnishings or grand decor. We could, however, keep our home clean and tidy.

Our dining service could not possibly afford the expensive gourmet delights. But we could work at improving the ambiance in our dining rooms.

We could challenge our frontline staff to a new level of gracious responses. A training program would be established.

We came away from our experience emboldened with optimism and determination.

However, the reality of our world soon came crashing in.

Our receptionist had kept guests waiting while she held a lengthy personal conversation on the telephone. The guests complained.

Our director of care enraged a family member when she suggested Dad's problem was not a neurological disorder but simply the result of alcohol abuse. The family member complained about her insensitivity and lack of respect.

The maintenance team left paint cans and brushes open in the nursing home hallway while they went for a meal. The resulting resident attempts at painting would take many hours to clean up. We all complained!

The personal support worker brusquely turned away a request from a family member with: "I don't have time for that." Another complaint.

It seemed that wherever we turned, we were performing at far less than the five star dream we had just experienced.

I shared our dream and our frustration with a trusted resident. He came back soon after with a small handwritten card. I still have it among my memorabilia.

"The Fifth Star is in the Details!"

We debriefed from our time together and the stresses of our first day back. We would continue to strive for our ideal, we would model the dream, and we would continue to raise the bar on service excellence for our staff. And we would stay tuned in to the details.

Did we succeed?

Over time those details were more quickly identified and addressed.

Staff mentoring and education continued unabated.

To quote a new resident: "We might not be luxurious. Who needs luxury? The service is second-to-none. We feel honoured and valued."

We have never afforded the privilege of a return visit to the hotel. However, we are still minding the details!

Lesson Learned

The Fifth Star is in the details!

What Is Required of Me?

T he dining services supervisor had been employed at Christie Gardens for several years. He was a big man with a strongly-felt presence. For some reason, he attracted criticism from his co-workers. Complaints of abrasive behaviour, aggressive directives, and the disruptive impact on the busy kitchen, especially just before meals, seemed to be without resolution.

The director of dining services didn't know what more she could do. She had tried challenging him, threatening disciplinary action, even potential loss of employment. He didn't acknowledge any performance failings and accused those complaining against him as being troublemakers.

He was a seriously unhappy man. There was no visible improvement in his behaviour, and the complaints escalated. It seemed there would not be peace with him present.

And so if fell to my lot, at the director's request, to "deal with him." The expectation was that I would dismiss him from employment.

These were heady days. Power rested in the hands of the leader. Employee rights were not readily protected. The employee would be at the mercy of the "big boss."

And so I asked that John come to my office. I had prepared my speech. We had experienced enough of his disruptive behaviour. His employment in our dining services was over.

John had always been polite to me. I had not observed the reported behaviours personally. He was also a capable part-time cook, often filling in when needed. And so, with some doubts lingering, I asked John to sit down.

As he did, I glanced up toward the framed quote on my wall. It had been a souvenir of a trip to Israel and was notable in that it was written in Hebrew and English. Its presence on my office wall had become normal. I rarely noticed it, let alone reflected on it.

The words seemed to jump as if spoken out loud.

It was an Old Testament quote from the King James Version of the Bible: "and what doth the Lord require of thee, but to do justly, and to love mercy, and to walk humbly with thy God?" Micah 6:8).

I knew without a doubt this message was for me — and now.

Had anyone considered these concepts when accepting and building on the complaints? Was there any mercy in the apparent solution? Were we missing justice entirely and being unduly influenced by a poisoned atmosphere? How about giving up the power and asking how I could help him?

I put the speech to one side and shared my feelings with him. He responded emotionally and shared with me his personal challenges. He was indeed a very distressed man. He acknowledged his behaviours had emerged as his personal difficulties escalated. We spent over an hour in discussion, exploring the options available and how we might help him.

It would be very gratifying to say we solved the situation that day.

Mercy, justice, and humility could be hard work. Addressing the discontent in the kitchen and the responses of his co-workers was also difficult.

We intervened actively when stresses built up and did not leave complaints untended. It would have been easier but a serious failing on my part as the leader to simply dismiss him.

A new leadership standard emerged from the experience. We would see John continue in our employ for three more years.

The lessons we were learning were to become a roadmap for the decision making processes into the future, and are part of the values statement of Christie Gardens to this day.

A simple wall plaque with a powerful message became a vital defining moment on the Joyful Journey.

Lesson Learned

"He hath shewed thee, O man, what is good; and what doth the Lord require of thee, but to do justly, and to love mercy, and to walk humbly with thy God?" Micah 6:8 (NKJV)

Christie Gardens
Life Lease

Architect's Concept for The Terrace at Christie Gardens.

Securing Our Future

1999

Christie Gardens was in its 15th year. Our house was fully occupied, and the interest in our apartments was increasing. We had noted, however, an emerging trend.

> Our apartments, at 600 square feet, were
> fully equipped, but for many potential
> renters were considered too small.

Couples often turned away disappointed as they reflected on the personal impact of a transition from their homes to such confined living space.

At the same time, our commercial kitchen was proving to be inadequate.

It had been designed to provide a meal service for 88 nursing home residents. However, we were now serving hundreds of meals more per day, with an increase in participation by our apartment residents and their guests.

Parking space, both indoor and out, did not meet the growing demand.

Building codes were satisfied, but our residents, staff, and guests were not pleased with only two elevators for our very busy house.

Our auditorium was too small, our office space sorely limited, and on and on went the list.

And our financial reserves were very limited.

We had learned of the success of another community in building and successfully marketing what was known as "Life Lease." This unique model used purchasers' funds to build, without incurring additional debt for the organization.

While the end result seemed like a condominium project, it differed primarily in its ownership arrangement. Legal language referred to the suites as having a lease-hold arrangement. I could understand it best as "purchasing the right to occupy the suite space, with ownership and operating responsibility staying in the hands of the board of directors. On resale, any increase in value would be to the advantage of the leaseholder."

It seemed like an enticing option to grow and improve our house. With the approval and encouragement of the board of directors, we began our explorations.

We did not have the privilege of land available on which to build. To meet the demands of future residents, and achieve the desired upgrades, we would be required to enlarge and renovate our existing building.

We contacted a recommended life lease consultant and an architect. They were eager and well equipped to serve us, but even after several meetings, we had made little progress. We felt constrained by our small plot of land and by building codes and zoning bylaws.

Once again, our creative visionary at the head of our board stepped up. Mr. Alexander, with pencil in hand and a sheet of newsprint on the table, sketched what he envisioned could be the footprint and future of Christie Gardens. That pencil sketch, remaining within the constraints of our land, became the inspiration for the final product, *The Terrace at Christie Gardens.*

And now, with full board approval, as we began our public announcements and marketing, we were faced with nay-sayers. "Too complicated," "purchasers would not risk investing in this new unregulated model," "the construction would be too much of a disturbance for our residents," and on and on. The underlying challenge seemed to be "who did we think we were?"

However, we had identified a need, saw an opportunity, measured the risks, and felt that, nay-sayers notwithstanding, we could move forward with this exciting project. Our plans were rooted in the philosophy shared years before by Mr. Alexander — that, fundamentally, we were called to serve those who called Christie Gardens "home" in an ever-changing world. We were confident that in so doing we would secure the future of Christie Gardens, and I knew that this would be another step on my Joyful Journey.

Lesson Learned

Never stop planning for the future. Change is good. Always remember your primary mission.

Grace Sweatman and David Sweatman, 2002.

The Permits!

January 2002

The Terrace at Christie Gardens had reached its sales target. We had successfully made our way through the complexities of bylaw and zoning changes and conducted the requisite public meetings.

We had survived an Ontario Municipal Board hearing launched by a neighbour who contended that our building addition would cast large shadows and diminish the value of the townhomes on nearby streets. The adjudicator denied the claim. The final hurdle had been overcome.

The City of Toronto had issued its building permit for excavation and foundation work to begin, a very exhilarating milestone. The hoarding was installed and major excavations begun. We were all very relieved that our audacious project was underway.

And then a major hiccup occurred.

While we were proceeding with our project, a well known developer in the city had acquired a multi-year lease on a valuable piece of waterfront land owned by the city. He then promptly resold the lease with millions of dollars of profit.

The resulting hue and cry became a political firestorm, with the blame for allowing this to occur resting on the city real estate department. Lawyers at the city's helm determined they would never again allow a "flip" of leasehold land.

We tripped into that scenario with our 99-year prepaid lease on our city-owned land.

Our relationship with the city had never been a concern. We were secure in the lengthy tenure of our pre-paid lease and our role as a not-for-profit charity.

Suddenly a spotlight was thrown on our application and approvals. Lawyers in the city advised the real estate department that they believed we were planning to sell the lease to a developer who would change the status to a private, for-profit corporation. They would not be "burned" again.

The call from the building department
was confusing and alarming.

"We have been advised that we must pull your excavation and construction permits. We believe the permits were issued by our department in good faith with all requirements fulfilled. However, we can only briefly resist their directive. You will need to meet with city lawyers and defend your position."

The hastily-called meeting with city officials, twelve of them and three of us, was a signal of their posture. It was clearly them versus us. The spokesperson, the head of the real estate department, made their position clear. They believed we were attempting a "flip" of the land and would be advising city council not to allow the project to proceed. The city councillor was present as an observer only.

My colleagues, our lawyer and consultant, spoke well but were met with stony disbelief and accusations. My composure was severely shaken. I spoke with a trembling voice and attempted to convince them they were wrong; we were the "good guys." We wanted to upgrade our building, enlarge our population, and enhance our services. We were not-for-profit and had every intention of remaining so. I then lost my composure and felt the tears coming, my dreaded sign of weakness.

The meeting ended soon after without resolution but with our request for a follow-up before they issued their summation to the city.

There was little handshaking that day.

The weeks following were a blur of sleepless nights and stress. The construction halted and big machines sat idle, causing many questions from residents and purchasers.

A colleague recommended we hire the services of a lawyer well known for her battles with the city on previous matters. She was very busy but agreed to review the file and join us in the planned follow-up meeting.

And so the second meeting occurred.

Their group was smaller but their position just as clear—they would not be approving the project and would be advising the city to withdraw the permits.

Our newly appointed lawyer spoke only once to the city representatives.

"You have a problem. You issued the permits, the project is underway, and grievous harm will be done to this not-for-profit group if you insist on withdrawing the permits. Why don't you just sell them the land for a nominal fee and resolve the matter once and for all?"

We left City Hall soon after. Her counsel to us was equally succinct.

"You have a very serious problem. I'd suggest you get ready to do a protest march down Yonge Street. You'll need public support to sway them. I wish you the best!" And that was that!

We had only two weeks before the dreaded council meeting. Our fate would be sealed. We would proceed, by some as yet unforeseen miracle, or we would be forced to cancel, return deposits, fill in the hole, and face as yet not fully understood but definitely grievous consequences. My fate and career would also be very uncertain.

When I refer to my Joyful Journey, this is part of the journey — the metaphorical "blown engine" or flat tire at the side of the road, far from a service centre. All we could do was wait.

Meanwhile, behind the scenes, unknown to us, there was much activity. Apparently the interdepartmental disagreement was heated, with the building department resisting the interference of the real estate department. Our city councillor was a strong supporter and spoke to me almost daily, offering encouragement and assurances there would be a solution.

Our councillor called me at home on Sunday evening. "Can you come to my office at City Hall for 9:00 tomorrow morning? The real estate department wish to discuss their final report with you." He gave no clue as to its content.

This time only our consultant and I attended. We were gravely concerned and spoke little. We waited outside our councillor's office feeling like children sitting outside a school principal's office waiting for punishment. The councillor welcomed us with an encouraging smile.

The meeting was brief and to the point. The spokeswoman, the head of the real estate department, read from her notes.

"We have reviewed the file and believe we have a solution. We will be recommending to city council that we change the lease-hold relationship by selling you the land for a nominal fee. Subject to council approval, we will remove our demand for the cancellation of your permits and you may then proceed with construction. There will of course be conditions, but based on what you have told us, I believe you can achieve them."

**Whew! The unforeseen miracle had occurred.
Once again, our councillor supported us seeking
final council approval, and the rest is history.**

Oh yes, one more step... the mysterious ownership of the land reflected in the sales agreements to date was no more. Christie Gardens was now, and continues to be, the rightful owner of the land.

The excavations resumed the next morning.

Lesson Learned

Stay the course.

Grace Sweatman, 2003

The Sky Is Falling!

1999 to 2002

Construction on the life lease addition to Christie Gardens had been underway for over a year. The major renovation would add three floors on top of the original seven-storey building, and build a ten-storey connecting tower from the basement up. It would also provide for major enhancements to amenity space.

The project was in fact a major rebuild of the whole building. We would be adding eighty-four Life Lease Suites, from 900 to 1,600 square feet, a new commercial kitchen, underground parking, a new auditorium, a completely rebuilt entrance foyer and lobby area, additional elevators, and indeed much more.

General contractors were reluctant to bid on what they considered to be a "renovation," citing the challenges of working around 300 seniors who lived there. They also felt it would be impossible to determine the cost.

The only other option available to us was to contract the services of a construction manager. This person would report to the owner/operator of the building, identified for the record as yours truly. Reporting to me was an experienced consultant who would co-ordinate between the architect and the construction manager.

In the fall of 1999, our enormous task began. In order to secure our building permit, we had faced public consultations for zoning changes, an Ontario Municipal Board hearing, which was deemed frivolous by the adjudicator when it finally reached a hearing, and ongoing financial concerns over the cost of the change notices!

In our first excavation to prepare for future underground parking, we discovered tons of concrete in pillars from a previous building. The resulting use of jackhammers for hours each day could well have caused upset for our residents. And yet it did not. To our pleasant surprise, there were no complaints from neighbours.

The excitement was palpable. Our purchasers, future residents, were eagerly awaiting the completion of construction. And they would indeed wait — through three formal delays in completion dates — while they planned their moves into our community.

The most invasive part of the project was the addition of three floors on top of the seventh floor, the top of the original building.

"Will the folk living in the apartments on the seventh floor be able to remain in their suites for the duration of the construction?"

"Yes," replied our endlessly optimistic construction manager. "I see no reason why not."

Comforted by his assurances, we offered these residents their choice whether to relocate to an apartment we could provide, or remain on the seventh floor while the construction proceeded

Seven brave souls of the fifteen residents living on the seventh floor decided to stay in their apartments for the duration of the construction. We soon realized his was hollow assurance.

If only we had known then what we quickly learned: the seventh floor would become an unsafe, noisy construction zone.

Construction materials and equipment to climb over. Loss of hallway heating. Frequent loss of lighting. Construction workers coming and going all day. Noise, noise, and more noise.

What no one clearly understood at the time was the impact on the existing building of the installation of the plumbing and heating systems for those top three floors. Nor could we have begun to anticipate the failure of the window company to deliver the new windows in a timely manner, in fulfillment of their signed contract.

In preparation for this vital component of the construction, the exterior roof had been stripped, the shell of the top three new floors of the new building erected, and the interior structure begun. We were ready!

And then, the window company did not meet their early November promised delivery and installation dates.

Nor their mid-November dates. Nor their early-December commitment. We were not high on their list. They had ongoing contracts with major developers. We were a one-time little guy with no influence. Assurances given by the window manufacturer were simply not fulfilled, again and again.

And then the unusual winter rains began.

Heavy and ongoing. In spite of the plastic sheeting covering the new superstructure, leaks into the building began with a vengeance. Each day the maintenance team and any one else available to assist would clean up the resulting water damage. One day they dealt with water leaks in 23 apartments.

"How many apartments today?" became a familiar refrain.

On Christmas day of 2000, we planned a celebration with families with a traditional Christmas dinner. With impeccable timing, no sooner had the residents and guests chosen their tables and were waiting for the feast, than the roof began to overflow into the beautifully decorated dining room.

Guests assisted the staff team in setting up an alternative in the hallways and lobby spaces. Residents were relocated to their new seats, and the celebration began again!

On another memorable day, the door to the elevator in the lower lobby opened and a wall of water poured out onto two nurses standing waiting. The shock was diminished somewhat by the fact that we had become accustomed to "what next?" It became an incident to laugh over. One more story to tell. Another part of the Joyful Journey.

No residents were harmed, or even got wet!
Just more water to clean up, and the loss of
one of our elevators for several days.

Remarkably, residents and staff did not respond to the extraordinary happenings with negative rumblings. Rather, they shared in the great adventure. One gracious resident opined that she didn't know what she would do when this ended. It was so exciting! Residents facing the front of the building would invite others in for afternoon tea so they could also enjoy a first-hand look at the construction, and the handsome crane operator.

In the midst of the frenetic activity, with each day bringing its new challenges, the receptionist received a call from an excited resident.

"My friend on the seventh floor asked me to call you.
She was sitting in her living room reading when a great
chunk of concrete from the ceiling landed beside her."

The distress level seemed a little higher than usual. The on-site project manager, my middle son, David, who had experienced many "happenings," took this one casually. "Oh really? Probably some dust from all the vibrations going on. I'm sure it's nothing to worry about."

Wisdom prevailed, however. "How about I check and make sure everything is ok?"

On his arrival at the apartment, he was greeted by a somewhat disheveled resident. "My ceiling is falling, and it just missed me!"

"Let's have a look, Mrs. Jones. Oh, there it is. Something did fall, but all else is ok. How about I take this with me so you don't have to worry about it any more. We'll send someone up this afternoon to fill in the hole."

Smart fellow. The ceiling had indeed fallen. Or at least a heavy chunk of three-inch-thick concrete, finished with ceiling stippling, had indeed just missed falling on her.

The sky was falling, or so it seemed!

That chunk of concrete became a reminder of a near miss, and a story many would share. We built a shadow box to house it. It remains on display to this day.

The windows finally did arrive in the spring of 2001. We welcomed our first life lease resident on April 1, 2003. The twenty-three million dollar project, all financed by the purchasers' investment in their new homes, became a never-to-be-forgotten chapter in the history of Christie Gardens.

The sky did not fall. We had no law suits, no injuries, no WSIB claims, no aggressive complaints, during the whole lengthy process.

Our purchasers fulfilled their agreements and we opened on April 1, 2003, fully Sold Out!

We continue to enjoy the fruit of that labour to this day. Would we do it again? Absolutely.

Lesson Learned

Would we recommend it to anyone else? Absolutely not.

Moving In

The construction project that would add 84 life lease suites to our continuing-care community had been underway for 18 months. Trusting seniors had paid their deposits, purchasing the right to occupy the space, condo-like suites of up to 1600 square feet. They had been given opportunity to choose their finishes and, in some cases, actually made modifications to the initial plans.

Delays had occurred: weather, late arrival
of windows, shortage of skilled tradesmen,
legal challenges via the OMB hearing.

We were feeling the stress, as were the elderly purchasers. Some purchasers were forced to cancel their agreements due to declining health.

Finally, with three notifications of delay behind us, we made the decision. We would begin receiving our new residents on April 1st. No "buts." We would not be delaying any further.

The architect overseeing the renovation and addition had worked diligently to satisfy building guidelines. She did not have the confidence that we could achieve that deadline, now six weeks away, but she would do her best to make it happen.

The construction manager, once overly-optimistic, abandoned that posture and regularly reiterated his message: "cannot be ready by that date."

There was, of course, the small
matter of occupancy permits.

We had already made what felt like a major concession when we agreed to floor-by-floor completion and inspection, rather than wait for occupancy approval of all 9 floors of suites at once.

Based on our decision to begin welcoming residents and their possessions, our first life lease resident, Miss Hutchinson, was advised she could move into her 2nd floor suite on April 1, 2003, now six weeks away.

Miss Hutchinson was relieved that her suite would be ready and was eagerly looking forward to moving in. We made the date very clear: April 1st, no sooner. She promptly listed her home and quickly sold it in the overheated city housing market. She then made her moving arrangements. Her negotiated closing date for her home sale was March 30.

Miss Hutchinson advised us of her need to come in a "little early." She would stay overnight with a friend on the 30th and would be arriving early on the 31st with the moving truck to take possession of her suite. She was certain this should be no problem. She was ready!

We were almost ready.

The serious remaining concern, however, was that the occupancy permit might not be in hand in time for our target date, April 1st, let alone her target date, March 31st.

After all we had been through, I couldn't fathom the excitement over this simple step. The architect, however, did not share my lack of concern. "Please do not allow anyone to take possession and move in to their suite without an occupancy permit. It is against the rules. Our architect's license could be imperilled."

And so now it was not the weather, the windows, absent tradesmen, or OMB hearings, but a simple piece of paper issued by a building inspector.

"These seniors have experienced three delays. They are experiencing dreadful stress. They have houses to sell, in some cases already sold!

We must give them dates. I'm concerned that if we allow more time, that new deadline will be just as difficult to achieve."

"Can you let her just move in her furniture, but not sleep there overnight?"

"I think we can negotiate this option. Leave it with me."

March 31st arrived and, as promised, so did Miss Hutchinson with her moving truck.

We created a welcoming celebration. Almost there! We then offered our very special new resident a complimentary dinner in our dining room.

Early in the evening, I visited Miss Hutchinson. The movers had caught the excitement and had done their best to set up her furniture and make her comfortable. Her bed was made.

"Welcome to your new home. We are so thrilled you're safely here. We have only one remaining matter to resolve. We do not have an occupancy permit for your suite. I'm obliged to advise you that you may not sleep in your suite tonight. However, in order to make you comfortable, we have a guest suite prepared and ready for you overnight. It's next to the elevator on the 3rd floor, very convenient and well equipped.

"Thank you so much, Mrs. Sweatman. It has been a long and tiring experience. I do understand your dilemma. I will bid you goodnight." She reached out her hand for the guest apartment key, and with an exaggerated wink, closed her door.

In the morning, following up on the well-being of our resident, we soon realized that the guest suite had not been disturbed.

We then made our way to the 2nd floor and Miss Hutchinson.

She answered her door dressed and ready for the day. "Good morning. I had a wonderful sleep, thank you. Thank you for all your efforts on my behalf." And once more, with an exaggerated wink, she handed us back the guest apartment key and closed her door.

Exhilarating days. Many challenges and surprises, but Miss Hutchinson set the tone!

She lived with us several years and loved to share her guest suite experience.

The final review of our construction materials and documents revealed a "miss." The critical occupancy permits had been authorized one floor per month.

In the great hurly burly of our unrelenting adventure, an occupancy permit for the 2nd floor had never been issued.

And the universe continued to unfold!

Lesson Learned

Sometimes reality, and service, trumps rules.

Faint Praise?

With the construction of the Terrace behind us, and with a (nearly) complete set of occupancy permits filed away in a cabinet somewhere, we moved forward.

My hard work had not gone unnoticed; in fact, I had been nominated for an award!

I had been nominated for an award in the category of Business, Entrepreneurial and Professional.

The nomination in itself had been a great honour. My nomination was submitted by a colleague based on my experience as the general contractor of The Terrace at Christie Gardens, the twenty-two million dollar project which enlarged and enhanced our now ten-storey continuing-care community serving seniors.

To actually be the chosen leader in my category was dreamt of, but never actually expected.

And so here we were.

The event was a great boost to my self-esteem, a luncheon in a banquet hall with three hundred guests in attendance. A table of eight, all my invited guests, at no cost to me. A young national Canadian organization called "Leading Women" was celebrating its third annual awards luncheon. Successful women, many of whom were well known leaders in their faith-based organizations, were present. It was a heady time and especially so for me. My guests were work colleagues and my daughters and daughters-in-law. They were all very kind and enthusiastic on my behalf.

There were four categories, mine to be presented last. The tone was set. As each honouree was presented, a video was shown of the recognized achievement with complimentary script by the hostess, the president of the Leading Women organization. The audio visual presentation was followed by the introduction of the award presenter, a recognized leader in her own right. Then would come the invitation to the actual winner to come to the podium.

By the time my turn came, I was feeling overwhelmed and not a little uncertain.

The other honourees appeared to me to all be gracious, well educated and informed, and worthy of the honour extended to them. Who was I in such august company?

My video had been prepared as part of the nomination application process. It presented well the four-year adventure of our development and construction project. Memories flooded and my confidence returned. It had indeed been an achievement in which I could take pride.

Before the luncheon I'd been invited to be interviewed by my chosen presenter. Mrs. Linda Tripp ("call me Linda") was a VP of World Vision Canada, the first woman to achieve that stature in the world-renowned organization. My introduction to her was in itself a great honour.

And so the moment I had been waiting for: "Grace Sweatman, would you please join us at the podium."

I made my way carefully and stood beside my presenter.

It was quickly apparent that Linda had earned her role as VP. She was a thoughtful, skilled speaker who had prepared well. The warm glow of success I felt was very satisfying. She presented my certificate, and photos were taken for posterity.

Just as I was preparing to "float" off the platform, Linda leaned into the microphone one more time.

"I will leave you all with one last thought. It was my honour to meet and talk with Grace before our luncheon. She is indeed a special leader worthy of this honour. I have identified one of the reasons for Grace's success. She does not suffer fools gladly!"

And with that summation, and the audience's response of laughter and applause, she shook my hand and hoped we would meet again. Together we left the platform.

The warm glow dissipated. The presentation and praise melted into her summation.

Me? Not suffer fools gladly? Whatever gave her that idea? I certainly had to consider that assessment.

The experience became an important lesson. Over the years when I was tempted to respond curtly to irritation or frustration, I would feel the "gut check." Not suffer fools gladly? Oh dear, Grace, be kind and gentle.

The framed certificate on my bedroom wall serves to remind me.

Lesson Learned

Thank you, Linda, for your insight and wisdom in sharing your perception, deflating as it might have been. Perhaps it is time we meet again! I trust your impression will be slightly altered should that meeting occur.

Leaving the System

Leaving the System, Part 1: Mission at Risk

April 2002

The most attractive feature of Christie Gardens, frequently cited by residents and their families, was the assurance that if their health status changed and full-time care was needed, they could receive that care in their own community, Long-term Care at Christie Gardens.

Throughout the province at that time, each home managed its own waiting lists. Some were in greater demand than others, due in no small part to the reputation of the home.

We had a well earned place in that group.

We had been successful in fulfilling our promise to our residents. The same promise imagined by Mr. Alexander and Mr. Wilkie so many years before. The 88 licensed long-term care "beds" were ample to serve the 335 residents living in our apartments and life lease suites, our "independent living suites."

Every vacancy in long-term care was being filled from our internal waiting list. Through careful management, we had maintained 100 per cent occupancy. However, external pressure for admission by non-residents was growing.

All was not well throughout the sector.

The families of frail elderly persons with complex care needs, or folk suffering from the effects of dementia, often had difficulty locating a home of their choice that would accept their loved ones as residents.

Typically, the most vulnerable were the last served.

There was a negative perception among officials in the Ministry of Health that some operators were "cherry-picking" applicants, admitting only those who required "light care." Little consideration was given to the reality of the shortage of beds province-wide

Our commitment to our residents meant we did not admit outside applicants to long-term care based on their care needs. We had promised! We were indeed "cherry-picking," only we would not have called it that! We simply served our residents.

We would accept only applicants who were already living independently at Christie Gardens and had become part of this community.

And then the thing we feared might happen, did happen. The Ministry of Health, with much fanfare, announced a new system. They made a series of pronouncements.

The "care" in long-term care was government funded; therefore, long-term care would be equally accessible by all, regardless of their care needs. A "central placement service" would be developed. In order to receive approval for care and be admitted to a long-term care home, the applicant must be approved and granted admission through the offices of Placement Coordination Services (PCS), later renamed Continuing Care Access Centres (CCAC). All contact prior to admission would be limited to that between government officials and the applicant. Admission would be to a home of the applicant's choice, not the decision of the operator. No operators would manage their own waiting lists.

This decision caused us grave concern. It appeared to be the worst sort of government "over-reach."

We could no longer assure access to Christie Gardens' long-term care for our residents. It was apparent there would be little or no recognition of our mandate. The government position was clear:

everyone would be entitled to move into the home of their choice, regardless of their current address or care needs.

We determined that we would resist the process for as long as we could while actively seeking a solution.

The first years in placement coordinating were very challenging for the newly hired Ministry of Health placement staff. They were empowered but not yet capable of implementing their new and untested policies.

They certainly did not anticipate, nor did they respect, the sense of ownership and personal responsibility felt by some of the homes, particularly in the not-for-profit sector.

We were not alone in our negative reaction to this legislation. Many of these homes were faith-based or served a cultural cohort. They had been developed by volunteers for this purpose. However, in this new reality, their history had no bearing on the mandate of the civil servants coordinating the admission process.

In this knowledge gap and inexperience on the part of the new civil servants, we managed to continue to maintain our own lists for a time.

We were a small player in a very large field, so we kept our heads down and did our best to avoid any spotlight.

And then the ruling political party of the day, in response to a now clearly identified shortage of available beds, made the decision to dramatically increase the number of long-term care beds in the province. Six thousand new beds would become available in the Toronto area alone.

While these new beds were being developed, the focus on placement became a secondary issue, easing the initial aggressive monitoring of the operators' admission practices.

By year six, however, the Ministry of Health teams empowered to manage the lists had become more proficient, they were making better use of technology, and the newly available beds had been quickly filled. We began to be aggressively challenged regarding our admission practices. Our period of "grace" had ended.

We were not obeying the law!

We were informed that no admissions would be approved unless they were chosen by the central placement service. We were reminded that applicants from our address must apply through the government agency with no special privileges.

Our right to admit applicants from our community was severely limited. There was no provision in the law for exceptions to the rules for continuing-care communities. Nor was there any support from the ministry employees. They had become advocates only for the perceived "underdog," the individual applicants living with high care needs.

Much frustration, barely contained anger, and on occasion deception, were becoming our lot as we continued with our determination to fulfill our commitment to our residents.

Our philosophy, indeed our mission, had never been simply a marketing strategy or a tag line; it was a deeply-held belief. Our commitment to our residents was a fundamental part of that mission.

We needed a solution, and soon.

Leaving the System, Part 2:
Mission Impossible

December 2008: The Moment of Truth

By year six of central placement, we had reached our moment of truth.

Mrs. Brown was a resident who had lived in her apartment at Christie Gardens for twelve years. She was a gracious 97-year-old who had committed her life to mission work in Japan. She was very well known and respected.

Mrs. Brown suffered a slight stroke and was admitted to hospital.

Once she had recovered sufficiently that she no longer needed acute care, she and her sons were advised by the hospital discharge planners that she could not return to her apartment.

She was told that she must choose five homes from the Toronto list of options in order to access long-term care services. "We won't have a problem," the family responded. "Our mother lives at Christie Gardens, and they promised she'd be cared for there if the need arose."

Much to their dismay, the response was definite and final. "Christie Gardens' waiting list is much too long; you must choose other options."

The moment of truth had arrived! Our director of resident services was dismayed. "How can I possibly tell the family that Mrs. Brown can't come home? Her friends will also be devastated and justifiably concerned for their own future as well."

Our purpose for being was seriously challenged.

We needed to resolve this dilemma for Mrs. Brown's and those who would follow her. The decision was made. "Advise her sons to inform the hospital that they have found a solution and that they will be taking her home."

Bring Mrs. Brown Home!

Mrs. Brown was admitted to Christie Gardens Long-term Care, without the required approval.

In the event of a future challenge of this decision, we would "face the music."

Meanwhile, with the full support of the board of directors, we hired a consultant and established a strategic planning committee. There were representatives from the board of directors, the team of operating directors, family members, and residents from "Independent Living," all determined to address and resolve this serious matter.

Indeed, we believed our very future hinged on its outcome.

The exercise took almost a full year with a final report and recommendations for consideration to the board of directors at its meeting in November 2009.

It was abundantly clear. Residents had chosen Christie Gardens for the assurance they would have access to full care *if and when needed.* We had a deeply-held belief that this was the best way to serve our community. This factor took precedence over any other. They would pay their own way.

One of our operating principles was that no one would ever be advised to seek services elsewhere for purely financial reasons. Therefore, we carefully considered how we might provide relief from the financial strain should the need for more care cause undue hardship.

Into this gap stepped the newly reactivated Christie Gardens Foundation with its benevolent fund, supported generously by its donors.

Christie Gardens would continue as a fully "self-funded continuing-care community."

Leaving the System, Part 3:
A New Path Forward

December 1, 2009

A defining moment in our history was underway. The board of directors made their decision and communicated to the Ministry of Health.

"We understand that in a publicly-funded system there can be no privileged access to care. For Christie Gardens to fulfill its mission and obligation to its residents, access to care must be privileged.

Therefore, the board of directors of Christie Gardens has made the decision to withdraw from the publicly-funded system.

We will see this process through by attrition. Effective immediately, each vacancy in our long-term care home will be filled from our internal waiting list.

Based on historical statistics, we anticipate this process will take approximately three years. Therefore, we will release our license as a government- funded care home on March 31, 2013, the end of our current operating agreement."

We would face this most complex transition with our mission and values intact.

To our knowledge, we were the first community ever to take this step. We were in previously uncharted territory. There were important principles to be maintained.

We determined that our residents would be best served as we implemented our decision if we conducted ourselves with transparency, diligence, and integrity.

We would communicate clearly and frequently to all involved.

We would honour the status of those currently living in long-term care.

No one would be asked to leave or face onerous fee increases.

We promised government officials the Ministry of Health would not suffer exposure or embarrassment.

This decision charted a healthy future for Christie Gardens.

We fulfilled our commitments.

We experienced consistent encouragement and support from our residents and their families.

We made a successful transition from a government-funded long-term care home to a fully self-funded continuing-care community, over the course of forty long months.

Whew! We had "brought Mrs. Brown home."

We enjoyed the pleasure of her company until her 100th year. Little did she know that she was a key player in the Joyful Journey: our final admission to government-funded long-term care.

Leaving the System, Part 4: SOLD!

December 2009

The Ministry of Health had been advised of our plan to withdraw from the publicly-funded long-term care system. We had begun intensive discussions with officials regarding our decision and intentions. We had provided assurances that no one would suffer harm in the process. We had done our best to assure Ministry of Health officials we would cause no media fallout. We would continue with our practice of high quality respectful care of our residents. Our decision was good news for all.

We now faced both an opportunity and a dilemma.

We had originally purchased our eighty-eight nursing home licenses from a private nursing home operator. These licenses were the legal mechanism for government funding for a long-term care home. Each license, or "bed" as they were often called, provided care for one individual. Operators were subject to rigid guidelines and an inspection process to assure ongoing funding.

There were no known legal impediments to the resale of these licenses. They were an asset that had no doubt increased in value. Resale of the assets was subject to approval by the Ministry of Health.

Our experience in the buying and selling of homes and licenses was limited to the original purchase in 1984. We had no relationship with a broker who could assist us. We certainly would need the income from the sale. We had no idea where to begin or how to see it through.

I mulled over this challenge and was uncertain how to proceed.

I decided I would proceed carefully, on my own, and make inquiries when the opportunity presented itself.

A week after our exciting announcement, I attended a Christmas dinner for the board of directors of the Ontario Long-Term Care Association. The evening had been promised as entertaining and engaging. The full restaurant had been reserved by our group.

The feature of the evening was the participation of the attendees in the preparation of the food for the dinner.

I had little interest in this kind of "fun" and decided I would work out of sight in the back kitchen where the potatoes would be peeled. My partner for this task was a fellow member of the board, a gentleman who had kindly mentored me when I was newly elected to serve. I had little experience or knowledge in the processes of a fully engaged, "working" board. My board tenure had been a unique and very satisfying experience. I trusted him. He was the president of a private corporation that owned and operated several homes in the city.

We began peeling what felt like a mountain of potatoes.

My "peeling partner" had heard of our decision to leave the system. He asked how we were faring. He felt we were very brave and wished he could do likewise.

In that kitchen, peeling potatoes and surrounded by wannabe chefs and the resulting cacophony of sound, I tentatively raised the subject of how I might proceed to sell the licenses. My fellow board member, mentor, and very successful colleague took a step back.

How many licenses do you have for sale?

Eighty-eight licenses.

When will they be available?

March 31, 2013.

How much do you want for them?

I quoted a price I had calculated as desirable based on the purchase price and appreciation.

He took a step back and reached out a gloved hand. "SOLD," he declared with a firm, potato-peel-encrusted handshake.

And that was that. They were indeed SOLD.

Others expressed interest. But the licenses were SOLD.

I was cautioned the deal would never close as it was too far into the future. But the licenses were SOLD.

I listened as detractors told me the Ministry would not approve a not-for-profit operator selling to a for-profit operator. But the licenses were SOLD.

Others told me he could just walk away from the $25,000 deposit his lawyer had advised. But the licenses were SOLD.

I suffered many anxious moments, but the licenses were SOLD.

My colleague kept his word. The Ministry of Health approved the sale. The funds received on closing of the sale provided a major boost to our cash flow. The licenses were indeed SOLD.

Lesson Learned

There is still a place in our world for trust and a handshake.

The Next Chapter

Catherine Belmore, Grace Sweatman, Colleen Lynas, Heather Janes, Kim Johnston, and Ed Clements, 2007.

Change: A Threat or a Blessing?

2007

We had begun the journey at Christie Gardens with a very matriarchal approach to our services. We were the "Mommas." We knew what was best for the seniors we were serving, and we cared about their well-being. So where could we possibly go wrong?

Dining services was the most measurable expression of this dynamic. When to eat, where to sit, with whom, and on what days was all dictated. If you missed a meal or were late for your sitting, we were sorry but your meal was lost! Looking back now, I'm somewhat surprised we didn't meet more opposition to our rigid policies.

Fortunately, two members of our leadership team had become accreditors (inspectors!) for the American accreditation process, which we had eagerly embraced. Their assignments took them to several states and gave them opportunity to observe other models of dining services. They would return from their assignments with fresh experiences and examples.

We realized we were behind the times in our operating approach and challenged ourselves to change.

The first step would be to change the approach to our dining service. "Open dining" were the new buzzwords. We would expand the dining room hours at each meal time. No more set times for the meal but whatever worked for you, on whatever days you preferred, and with whomever you chose as table-mates. We announced our plans well in advance and communicated the good news to our resident family.

To our surprise, the responses were overwhelmingly negative.

"How will I know where to sit?"

"What if someone takes my favourite seat?"

"How will I keep track of my fifteen meals?"

"How can I be sure I can sit with my friends?"

"There will be chaos in the dining room!"

There was talk of a petition.

The "buzz" was reflective of discontent. Letters began arriving, sometimes several a day, often with similar wording — a new experience in my leadership.

We continued on our course and attempted to dissuade the almost overwhelming negativity.

We would put an electronic tracking system in place that would facilitate the record keeping and provide opportunity for billing for additional meals.

We would select dining room supervisors who knew the residents well and could satisfy their table placement concerns.

We listened, smiled a lot, and had the courage to stand our ground while at the same time addressing the concerns.

We felt strongly that this small step to restore some autonomy and improve our dining service was critical to future success.

The momentous day arrived — dinnertime on a Thursday, the beginning of a new month. The dining team made it a celebration and wore their special uniforms. In The Courtyard, our long-term care home, the team had approached each resident to discuss their time and table companion preferences. We had done our best to address every concern.

Providing more autonomy was proving to be very challenging.

The rumble of conversation in the lineup for the main dining room could have been alarming.

A video of the residents of The Courtyard coming, with full staff support, to their chosen time and table was the most telling. Long, unhappy faces, muttering, and overall serious discontent. A definite change in their usual demeanour. Certainly not the celebration we had envisioned.

"Change? Why? What was wrong with what we had?"

"I don't want my lunch at a different time. I don't want to sit with someone different."

Even this most involved staff team expressed their concerns. They did not like change either.

The meal time did pass — or using a familiar expression: the universe did continue to unfold. The dining services team excelled as they escorted the residents to the table of their choice. The residents began to relax. No major incidents occurred.

We waited anxiously for the next unstructured mealtime. And the letters began again!

"Thanks for the new meal times and dining approach. I loved it and so did my friends."

"Please accept our apology for our negative reactions and thanks for staying firm. We are delighted."

"Please forgive my active resistance. Change is often threatening, you know."

"You were right. Sorry we gave you such a hard time."

Whew!

I am delighted to report that the changes we made very positively impacted our dining services, from structured institutional mealtimes to fine dining.

Our dining room is always very busy. Residents enjoy the flexibility and enjoy many more meals. The buzz of conversation reflects the overall comfort. New residents are warmly welcomed. We regularly serve many guests.

Close to the end of the month there is not a seat available as residents use up their meal quota.

In The Courtyard, where our most frail residents are served all of their meals, most of the residents and their staff support reverted to the patterns they knew. Their comfort was secure in the familiar. However, as new residents moved in, the fact that they could choose their mealtimes mattered.

The "Mommas" learned also. Change was indeed very threatening. Group stresses could emerge with inordinate negative reaction. Autonomy was invaluable, and wherever possible, lifestyle decisions would be best made by those who would experience the impact.

Underlying the experience was the reminder
that trust was critical to the quality of life
between the leaders and the residents.

Lesson Learned

*Once a decision has been made, carefully manage the outcomes but
stay strong. Change will always be a challenge.*

A Private Room, Please

Twenty years into my tenure at Christie Gardens, we were serving an extraordinary resident population of four hundred and twenty older persons in our ten-storey building. The success of our commitment to flexible accommodation and services depended on excelling in our capacity to respond effectively at time of greatest need.

Into this picture, with a record of ongoing full occupancy and lengthening waiting lists, came a challenge to our success: the demand for private rooms.

An endless conundrum in the operation of our nursing home was the demand for, and limited availability of, private rooms.

Who actually "needed" private rooms?

As far as the residents, and their families and friends, were concerned, all the nursing home residents did.

How could three or four elderly persons live together in harmony in very limited space?

Not easily; in actual fact, seldom.

Why did residents from the suites, floors 2 through 10, or the retirement home, on the first floor, so actively resist relocation to a semi-private or ward room in the nursing home when they were facing a critical need for the care?

Imagine how you would feel if your friend or loved one needed care and there was only a semi-private or ward room available. The sense of finality and loss could seem overwhelming.

The Courtyard, as our first floor was identified, was home to one hundred and twenty elderly residents, thirty-two of them in the retirement home, eight-eight in the Ministry of Health funded nursing home

The retirement home residents all enjoyed private rooms.

In the nursing home, only twenty-one residents enjoyed private rooms. The remaining nursing home residents lived in semi-private or three-or- four-bed ward rooms.

This room configuration resulted in unrelenting challenges for nursing home residents and the staff serving them. We struggled with the ongoing impact of stressful incidents and complaints and knew we must seek resolution.

Time was set aside for the review, and the leadership team began considering what options, if any, were available to us. Our resulting plan was very exciting.

As our first step in response to the needs of our apartment and life lease residents, rather than encouraging a move to the retirement home, we would deliver a roster of comprehensive support services to their suites. Residents choosing these services at a time of need could continue to thrive "at home."

As the private rooms in the retirement home became available, we would reclassify them as nursing home rooms. We would then transfer residents from their current semi-private or ward room in the nursing home to their new private room, thereby gradually phasing out the retirement home.

Over time we would reduce the population on the first floor from one hundred and twenty to eighty-eight persons, all nursing home residents, now living in expanded accommodations.

No renovations would be required.

It sounded complicated, and it was going to be, but well worth the effort and any risks.

The financial impact was carefully addressed with the conclusion that the plan would be expensive during the transition, but definitely possible. Could we afford the investment?

Our plan was readily approved by the board of directors. It was good news for all concerned. We would make the investment to see an effective resolution of this conundrum and continue in our commitment to serve our residents with excellence.

And then came the anxious question: Would we need the permission of the Ministry of Health for this undertaking?

I felt very strongly that this permission was not needed.

The plan we would be implementing enlarged the living space for the nursing home residents. It solved the unfortunate conundrum of the inadequate supply of private rooms. No renovations would be required. We would receive no additional funding from the Ministry for our investment.

We were the "good guys" here!

There was ongoing anxiety, however, among my senior leadership team over my decision to neither inform the Ministry nor seek permission.

"The next time the inspector comes, I'll tell her and give her a tour. Don't worry."

I was acquainted with our inspector and was confident I would meet no opposition to this initiative.

Some months later, with our plan well underway, came the fateful call. "A Ministry of Health inspector is here for a visit."

Yes, she was. But it was not our regularly assigned inspector, but a temporary replacement, and with a trainee in-tow!

So much for my plan to inform. A stranger to inspect our home! Someone accompanying her! There would no doubt be posturing and fault-finding as she modelled the how-to of inspections. This was simply not a wise time for disclosure of our ongoing transitions.

The next two days were very stressful for our leaders. Our inspector appeared indeed to be posturing for her trainee, and rather than a collaborative approach to the inspection, was highly critical throughout.

There was a complete absence of commendation for what we believed was a well-run home.

The inspector prepared her final report and presented it to the administrator and director of care. She had little in the way of actual "findings," just an overall critical attitude. A thoroughly stressful experience.

Once the ordeal was over and the inspector and her trainee had left our home, my colleagues came to my office to provide feedback. They were very distressed, close to tears.

From my safe haven, I expressed an entirely different response.

"Ladies, I am so sorry you had this experience. However, rather than sharing your distress, my jaw is aching from grinning. Our seasoned inspector, who apparently was trying to make you an example for her trainee, completely missed the fact that the nursing home she inspected was missing twelve of its residents."

They were now living, and being cared for, in their new private rooms down the hall!

My leaders would not be mollified. My safe haven had spared me but had not protected them. Throughout her visit, they had experienced ongoing concern. What if she discovered what we'd been doing without their knowledge? I had not kept my promise. I had failed to disclose our activities to the authorities!

Although I was entitled to take the lead in the risk-management, it seemed I had erred in my lack of consideration for the concerns of my colleagues.

The outcome?

I did move expeditiously to invite the regular inspector to visit. I prepared a presentation of the problem, the planning, and the very desirable outcome. She responded well, albeit with some surprise that we would have proceeded without their permission. She did support us, however, resulting in a belated letter of approval from the Ministry of Health.

The services to the independent living suites were, and continue to be, a very successful service option easily replacing the retirement home.

The private rooms for nursing home residents continue to be an immeasurable blessing.

The two remaining semi-private rooms, converted from what had been large ward rooms, are a highly desirable option for couples.

The old adage, often quoted, "better to seek forgiveness than ask permission" did not apply. No wrong had been committed. There was no need for forgiveness. We owned both the problem and the solution. And therein lies the heart of the risk management process.

Identify the problem; research thoroughly; make a plan; identify the risks; get it done; and own the outcome.

Lesson Learned

The solution rested with me.

Up From the Ashes of Failure!

A colleague inquired about my well-being. After expressing the normal platitude of "I am fine, thank you," I did acknowledge that, to my frustration, I was experiencing unrelenting fatigue.

"You need a personal trainer. I have a young man who comes to my workplace every week. He did a personal assessment and prepared a program of exercises tailored solely to address my areas of physical weakness. I've renewed my energy and feel great!" He then proceeded to reinforce his message with a vigorous sales pitch that I should at least meet him and consider this option.

And so, with many unresolved misgivings, I arranged an appointment with the young gentleman.

He was very personable and professional. He had a well-established client base but still had some time available. I decided that if he could make the time, he should meet our leadership team as well. They might be interested in this as an employee benefit.

Over the next few weeks, Jeff visited each director and prepared personal exercise plans and lifestyle recommendations. They seemed pleased with his counsel, and five of the six of them were prepared to give it a try.

I left my assessment until the last, still feeling very reluctant.

When finally faced with the outcome, there were no surprises. I needed his expertise and a plan to address my fatigue. He was most gracious and encouraging. I supposed I could give it a try. For the first week I applied his directives very diligently. I met him again in week two and considered how I might proceed.

And then I began to "fret." I felt daily concern over "failing."

I felt the constraint of additional commitments. How could I encourage my staff team when I could barely proceed myself?

He came at the appointed time on week three.

"Jeff, I have no doubt you are correct in your assessment and the recommended activities I should undertake. However, I am sorry, but this is not for me."

And then, without giving him opportunity to craft a rebuttal, I asked my key question.

"How would you feel about working with seniors?"

"I don't have a lot of experience with this group, but I can learn and would love the opportunity!"

Thus we began a unique program of activity, supplementing physiotherapy, and replacing the exercise programs then underway.

Today, two-thirds of our residents are served through the Christie Garden's Fitness Program, with a theme of "Let's Keep Moving!"

The fitness programs are enhanced by personalized assessments for newcomers and regular follow-up. The "house" buzzes with activity five mornings a week. The fitness team has grown to two full-time personal trainers and their two part-time trainees. There are currently five levels of participation available, from seated through to more advanced exercises.

This team collaborates successfully with the physiotherapists, who address more critical needs. Residents transition back and forth between the two disciplines as needs change.

We are assured regularly by resident participants that their quality of life has been enhanced through active participation in this program.

My position remains unchanged, however: not for me! Instead, I would address my fatigue through some practical lifestyle changes and believe this challenge could also be overcome. While a personal trainer was not my solution, it certainly has proven beneficial for many.

Onward.

Lesson Learned

"Up from the ashes of [my] failure grew the roses of success!"
(Henry Ford)

Difficult Realities

The group of eight gentlemen, members of a board of directors of a not-for-profit seniors community, had driven for four hours from their home in Southwestern Ontario to visit Christie Gardens. They had requested my advice regarding their options for the future of their seniors' apartments and potential purchase of a small long-term care home.

Their request was not uncommon. Christie Gardens was perceived to have been successful

in its unique approach to eldercare. This group hoped they could learn from our experience.

Our visit together turned into a five hour tour, luncheon, and brainstorming session. I would have been pleased to report that my investment in this group had been useful and inspiring. The actual experience did not appear to be so.

We extended our hospitality, introduced our guests to staff and residents throughout our tour, and enjoyed an excellent lunch together. And then we sat together to "brainstorm."

As an introduction to our afternoon conversation, I asked for a history of their home and their potential plans. Two of the gentlemen took on the task.

Their recounting became a lament of being misunderstood in their attempts to do good. It evolved into a rant against local politicians and "small-minded" townspeople.

They were facing constant complaints. Their rents were too high. Their building was in poor repair. Their staff were uncaring and rude. Their parking was insufficient.

They were dealing with difficult realities.

Their occupancy levels were less than 80 per cent. Their government relationship was poor and contentious. Their leader and staff were disgruntled. And what were they doing about it? A children's song flew unbidden into my mind.

"Nobody likes me. Everybody hates me. Guess I'll go eat worms!"

Some small voice of wisdom helped me not to quote it!

As far as I could see, their responses had become hostile and defensive.

Why were the rents too high? They explained that they had to meet their budget; there was no choice. They would have to raise them further if they had any hope of remaining viable.

Why was the building in poor repair? Well, that was the fault of the builder, and they couldn't afford to fix it up.

And the uncaring and rude staff? It was not their fault. The team was underpaid and tired out.

Where was the leader when theses complaints were made? He was the cause of many of the complaints.

What about the parking? There was nothing they could do.

And the occupancy? Their occupancy levels were at 80 per cent, a real concern but no idea how to address the matter.

The relationships with town leaders? They were just small-minded politicians.

Unhappy leader and staff? They could quit!

And they wanted to add a nursing home to that situation?

Yes, they believed all would be solved if they could provide "access to care" as we had done.

A distant dream, the solution to all their woes. If they could not manage a seniors' apartment building, how could they possibly operate a nursing home?

I do not recall a more frustrating conversation. Every suggestion was met with an excuse or reason why my idea was not possible.

There was not a glimmer of hope that I could see.

I finally drew the conversation and long day to a close.

"Gentlemen, you need to review your purpose for being. You must seriously address your current challenges. You need a shift in attitude toward your residents. You need a fresh review of your expectations of your leader. You need to paint your building! You need to get your house filled. Then and only then can you begin to consider your future options."

**I ended our day on the most positive
note I could muster.**

"Gentlemen, this was a tall order, and I trust you will accept it in good faith. Once you have taken definitive action, I encourage you to have another serious conversation.

Start afresh. Clarify your purpose for being and your true vision for the future. Consider your options carefully, the opportunities and the risks. Set your goal and 'go for it.'

When you meet an obstacle, climb over it and carry on. Few will stand in the way of determined leadership. I wish you the best."

Would that I had sensed gratitude for the tour, free lunch, and full day invested in addressing their quandary ... or some sense of "let's do it."

The gentlemen left for their long drive home with their lament still uppermost in their minds. And I left for my commute home, exhausted and deflated.

Was there a magic outcome?

I had heard negative murmurings by others in the area and was uncertain of their status. Failure would not have surprised me. However, as I did my research in preparation for this story, I was surprised by what I learned.

They did in fact purchase the small nursing home. They have recently been awarded additional beds by the Ministry of Health and are building a new nursing home. Their website reflects a positive outlook, excellent service, and skilled leadership.

Perhaps some day I'll have the pleasure of learning whether my challenge was part of their recovery. Meanwhile, it appears that they changed direction, made a plan and are carrying on.

Where there is life, there is hope!

The following action plan, given careful consideration, is a template for success:

- Check your motivation.

- Fix your foundation.
- Set your direction.

These thoughtful directives became a template for an important challenge we would face in our future.

But that is another story.

Lesson Learned

Where there is life, there is hope.

A Bold Call to Action

Something Was Not Working

What can you do when you realize your
unrelenting efforts are not resulting in
the long sought after outcome?

For 25 years I had devoted my career, energies, and in many ways, my life, to the unrelenting pursuit of "excellence" in the provision of flexible accommodations and services for the 420 residents who chose Christie Gardens as their home. The most heart-challenging focus had been on the care of our most frail residents. This group of 80 residents lived in The Courtyard, our full care home.

The evidence of our commitment?

Were we generous? Often to a fault.

Were we kind and gentle? Sometimes to the point of seeming weak.

Did we take risks? Whatever we believed was necessary to achieve our goal.

Did we obey the rules for quality care, as prescribed by others? We tried, even in the face of what sometimes seemed illogical.

Were we fully engaged in the lives of the people we served? Yes, as much as was possible.

The Outcome?

The dream of a continuing-care community had been fully realized. Flexible services, if and when needed.

Our marketing slogans were still part of our identity:

"Home for the rest of your life."

"The last and best move you will ever make."

"The best in town!"

"A kind and gentle place."

Our "House" was full with increasing demand for our services. We had become the residence of choice for many professionals and their friends and acquaintances from the city. Word of mouth was all we needed in marketing.

Our Services?

The Courtyard, our long-term care floor, underpinned our services. We were proud of our excellent care. Residents were clean, comfortable, and well-groomed. Our dining service was dedicated to fine dining for all the residents. Our staff were qualified. Our education of staff was ongoing. Our staffing level was the envy of other operators. Our caregivers had lengthy tenure, many of them more than my 25 years. Our leadership team was experienced and actively engaged in fulfilling our mission.

And yet, something was not working.

Over a period of several months, I had become increasingly concerned about the responses to the care needs of our residents. I had observed what felt like a nonchalance, even a benign neglect, as staff responded to residents' needs and expectations. I had observed healthcare-driven solutions when what appeared to be needed was respectful social engagement.

I began to hear family murmurings of discontent.

And for the first time in many years, I received a formal letter expressing concern on behalf of a friend, a recent admission to The Courtyard.

The source, nature, and content of the letter was entirely unexpected ...

Lesson Learned

Pay close attention to letters of complaint.

My Friend

December 2012

The letter was from a small group of long-time residents, written to express their concern on behalf of our mutual friend and resident, Miss Anne Johnson.

Their letter was not harsh; if anything, it was apologetic in tone. The authors made no demands; no threats were issued. For some reason I don't fully understand, it "hit" me harder, perhaps because it was expressed with kindness.

First, some background.

Miss Johnson was in her nineties. She had lived in an apartment at Christie Gardens for several years. Miss Johnson had successfully managed a life-long disability that impaired her mobility, increasingly so in recent years. She was using a wheelchair throughout the day.

I had a deep respect for Miss Johnson.

She was a kind, thoughtful lady. She only ever expressed positive comments about her home, her friends, and the staff who served at Christie Gardens. She was well known, well liked, and actively engaged in many of the groups and programs.

With no apparent warning, Miss Johnson experienced an infection that not only robbed her of her ability to use her wheelchair, but rendered her completely immobilized due to loss of strength in her arms and legs. She was suddenly fully dependant on others for all her needs. Ongoing full day private care was not an option that she could afford. She had a crisis need for the services of The Courtyard.

Rising to the Challenge

Miss Johnson became an immediate focus of concern for the leaders. We were very relieved when, within a few days, a small private room became available for her. Her family and friends, all elderly themselves, rallied to set up the room for her and took the steps to give notice on her apartment.

We were feeling quite satisfied with our timely ability to respond. We had fulfilled our ongoing commitment to provide alternatives if and when needed.

And then came the letter.

I received the letter about five days after she moved in. I had inquired about Miss Johnson and had been assured the staff team were doing all they could to care for her, and she indeed required full care.

I read the letter with mixed emotions. On the one hand I was concerned that the friends felt it had to be written. On the other hand, I experienced surprise and disappointment at their seeming lack of gratitude.

The ladies writing had taken great care to first express their appreciation. They then expressed their concern that Miss Johnson was struggling with the response to her needs. They felt she had lost more than her mobility. Her "person" was buried in the routines, schedules of the care givers, and the completely inadequate room in which she was now living.

One reaction could be to provide a response with the assurance that their concerns would be addressed, and then to pass on the letter to the director of resident services. This response seemed inadequate, however. Immediately upon reading the letter, I left my office and went to visit Miss Johnson.

Our Visit: An Ultimate Defining Moment

My visit that day became the ultimate defining moment of my career.

I arrived at her room feeling somewhat apprehensive about what I might find. What was initially evident to me was that our principles of care had been fully implemented. However, my experienced eye revealed that we were failing badly, in spite of our tendency to self congratulation.

Miss Johnson was well dressed and groomed. She was sitting in her wheelchair facing the door of her room. She was in a room that looked out on the garden. It was bright and clean. Her personal treasures were on her bureau.

But!

Miss Johnson could not enjoy the scenery, as her back was to the window, and the room was too small for the chair to be turned around.

Her call bell was fastened to the back of her chair in the event she needed assistance. There was no way she could reach the cord to pull the call bell.

Her personal support worker entered the room to check on her well- being.

She spoke to Miss Johnson at a volume that implied she was hard of hearing. Miss Johnson had no hearing loss.

She referred to her as "dearie." My friend had only ever been "Miss Johnson."

When the caregiver realized I was in the room, she apologized and said she would return. She had fulfilled her duties in a kind and friendly manner, but had missed the essence of the "person" of my friend.

I knelt in front of Miss Johnson and expressed my concern for her. The next few moments will not be forgotten.

Miss Johnson burst into tears. "I feel so completely helpless. Especially when they take me to the bathroom. I'm treated as if I were a little child with my nanny teaching me to pee!

"They think I'm deaf. They talk baby talk to me. They decide everything for me.

"Mealtime is really difficult. They bring me out to wait for the meal half an hour before it's ready, because they have many others to care for as well. They feed me at their pace, along with three others.

"They take me to programs, whether I'm interested or not, telling me it will be good for me.

"Mrs. Sweatman, I know they are kind and doing the best they can, but I cannot live like this."

By now we were both in tears.

I comforted her and promised I would do everything in my power to make it better for her. She thanked me for caring about her, and I left her room, thoroughly shaken.

The friends were right.

Our dream was not being fulfilled. The quality of Miss Johnson's life was seriously lacking in many areas. And on my watch!

My leadership team and I had learned of an urgent need, we solved the problem, monitored the situation, and were sure that we had it "right." And ye we were missing the mark.

Had I advocated all these years to realize this outcome? Wasn't the Journey toward excellence?

Lesson Learned

Keep an open mind. Avoid self-congratulation.
"Keep a weather eye."

A Turning Point

December 2012

O n my return to my office, I picked up my pen and writing pad and began to write what I would later call my Manifesto. A big word suitable for big feelings. Without stopping to consider grammar or presentation, I wrote rapidly, feeling overcome with sorrow and frustration, as indeed I was. The words just tumbled out. I wrote with passion.

The resulting expression of my feelings and sharing them with others became the communication tool that began a dramatic culture change in The Courtyard.

My first call was to the director of resident services, my youngest daughter who was herself already an experienced leader in our shared industry.

"Miss Johnson needs a larger room, now." Heather had no idea of what prompted my demand and was surprised and even resistant to my request.

"Why her? Why now?"

I invited her to my office to hear the reason for this demand. We spent the next hour reviewing my observations, hearing of Miss Johnson's distress, and listening to my Manifesto. Heather shared my heart and pain.

We then determined together that the future would be very different for our residents, beginning immediately.

We would work to see a dramatic change in the culture of our home. We realized it would be very complex and could take some time, but we would begin and never let up until we were satisfied with the outcome.

This journey became the reason for "Joyful." The next two years, indeed until my retirement from my role as CEO, were the most satisfying I could have experienced.

We implemented a successful initiative in culture change that is ongoing.

Lesson Learned

Make the best of these defining moments. They may make the difference between ordinary and extraordinary.

A Bold Call to Action

December 2012

Do you see me? Do you know who I am?

Am I a list of diseases, disabilities and prescriptions, behaviours, someone to manage?

How far down that chart you read do you have to go to see ME?

Do you know that I was a social activist and advocate for others all my life?

Do you know that my parents were missionaries to China and that I spent my working life in service to others?

Did you know that I am still working on my PhD while I struggle with advancing Parkinson's disease?

Do you know that I was a Bell Telephone supervisor for many years and that I wish there was something you could give me to do to help you?

Do you know that I am a father, grandfather, and overall nice person who fell to the ravages of Alzheimer disease? When you took me from my wife and brought me to a strange place with strange people all trying to tell me what to do, was "chemical restraint" the only solution available for you to manage me?

Did you know I just wanted you to dial the phone number for my daughter because I am almost blind, when you told me you do not have time for that kind of "stuff"?

Did you know when you picked up the metal tray from beside my bed and left the room that I had spilled the juice all over my nightclothes and that I was shivering with cold?

Did you know how much it frightened me when you put me in the standing lift and then wandered off to get someone to help?

Did you know that when I am calling out there are things I need that I am unable to express?

Why do you wear gloves when you come to help me? Do I have some kind of a contagious disease?

Why do you talk to each other instead of to me?

Do you see where I live?

This is the only private space that I have, my home!

Could you live in 140 square feet? Does 200 square feet sound better somehow?

I can't see the view out my window because I cannot manage my wheelchair and there is no room to turn it around.

Do I have to live in an institution with the noises, smells, and equipment as reminders?

Why are there carts in my hall and noisy deliveries going past my bedroom door?

Does anyone know, or care, how much personal dignity I have lost when it is made apparent I should use the incontinent products rather than be helped to the bathroom?

What about the washroom? Is there not some way I could have a shower in privacy and not have to be trundled through the halls wrapped in a bathrobe announcing to the world that it is "bath-time"?

Do you understand who serves me?

Are they committed to my quality of life or theirs?

Do they take my counsel or do they know best?

Do they take ownership of the challenges I face or put in their time and go home?

Are they "too busy"?

Is the activity of the day determined by their schedule or mine?

Why do I feel afraid to ask for help?

Do they see me? Do they know who I am?

Lesson Learned

Never fear sharing your heart!
Providing you have earned the right to be heard.

A Better Way

Changing the Culture
of Eldercare:
There is a Better Way

December 2012

The operating directors at Christie Gardens were a seven-member team of trusted, experienced, and dedicated leaders. Identifying and implementing "A Better Way" would require their support and active engagement. Immediately following my discussion with Heather, we extended a request for an urgent meeting in my office.

They heard my Call to Action and the account of my experience. It was as if a breath of relief flowed through the room. Together we owned this challenge and opportunity. We had survived on self-congratulation, believing that the service we provided was exemplary, but we were all sensing a need for significant change.

Our first step was to "Check our Motivation."

We had come to a crossroads in our efforts to care for the residents in The Courtyard. Were we simply "fighting fate"? Others had tried, time and time again. Every media-exploited incident in the care of residents in nursing homes became a catalyst to investigations, legislation, and inspection. It also widened the breach between the operators and their families. The perception of the public was that we were the enemy who must be monitored and managed.

One of our firm beliefs expressed whenever we had an audience was, "No amount of legislation can produce a high quality of life. The commitment to this ideal must come from the hearts of the leaders."

Our challenge was to be certain that this ideal was understood and owned by all, and to convince others that the hearts of these leaders were indeed fully committed to changing the culture of care of their loved one.

We had been given a sacred trust. We would do everything in our power to fulfill it in a way that enhanced the quality of life of the elders we served. There was a better way.

The second step was to "Fix our Foundation."

We were determined to truly define the cause of our failure.

What were the underlying issues that must be addressed before we could see a new way forward? Under no circumstance could we return to the model of care that was failing our residents and their families.

We knew our posture must change. Not the patronizing idea of how lucky you were to live in the Courtyard at Christie Gardens, but how privileged we were to serve you.

What constructive steps could we take to be sure the elders we served knew only respectful, high quality care, no matter their circumstance?

The third step was to "Set our Direction."

This would become our action plan. We determined we would be unrelenting in our pursuit of quality care for those who had entrusted their lives to us. We would "Change the Culture of Care" at Christie Gardens.

And so we began.

That fateful day ended with the directors calling an urgent meeting of the support staff team. This group of fifteen leaders serving in every department were the folk we trusted to address our concerns, identify solutions, and effect change. The challenge was mine to communicate my experience once again and share my Call to Action.

It was a very emotional experience. The Call resonated very strongly. The team sensed that this was a critical moment in our history and that the directors were united in their determination.

We then called a full staff meeting for the next day. Our request to the support staff team was that the purpose of the meeting would be kept confidential.

The next morning a visibly anxious group of close to 100 members of our staff team gathered in the auditorium. They couldn't imagine why they had been called together.

Once again the challenge was to communicate my experience, the writing of the Call to Action, and our determination to see a major shift. Feelings and promises, or indeed threats, were not going to achieve our desired outcome. Together we would determine the future for those we served.

The Journey had begun.

The directors collaborated throughout the day, responding to many questions and concerns from our staff, especially those responsible for the direct care of the residents.

Each director committed themselves to own the aspect most closely identified with their portfolio.

Action Plan

Our first formal initiative was to invite stakeholders from every area of our services to join us for a full day of discussion, discovery, and determination as we began our journey.

Included in this group were the leadership team members filling the role of host for our guests. Joining them were members of our board of directors, service providers and consultants from many venues, an architect, a labour representative, family representatives, residents, and staff.

The results of our day were carefully documented. They became the template for the next two years as we moved forward ...

Lesson Learned

It takes engagement from all stakeholders to create real change.

Changing the Culture
of Eldercare:
Discoveries and Decisions

December 2012

The all day meeting with stakeholders proved itself to be worthwhile and productive.

Step One — Our model of service reflected institutional
health care. Our residents were "patients" with
the primary focus on health and safety. Health

care staff decided what was best for them in their day to day living and when it should occur.

Understanding the importance of language, we would change our verbiage from "patients" or "seniors," expound on the meaning of the term "elder," and begin using it immediately.

We would empower the residents to decide what gave meaning to their day and how it could be achieved.

Step Two — **The supervisors were nurses who were responsible not only for health care, but staff management and much administrative responsibility.**

We would develop a plan that would "let the nurses nurse" and others take responsibility for day to day oversight.

Step Three — **Our service was marked by the constant messages of "too busy, hard work, too many residents, too many rules."**

The weapons of supervision tended to be threat and fear. Primary care givers, our personal support workers whom we now call "care partners," had a very demanding assignment, that of the care of ten or eleven residents.

We would change the day to day responsibility of resident care from an assignment of up to eleven residents to that of five or six residents.

We would move from "the rules" to empowering the care partner to respond to elder requests and needs.

Step Four — Our service resulted in many departmental silos, with frequent stresses between departments and a clearly expressed organizational hierarchy.

Elders experienced frequent invasions of their private space as various staff members fulfilled their assignments. There was little opportunity to build relationships with other residents or with staff members.

We would achieve the reduction in resident assignment by changing the duties of the primary care givers to include engagement in all aspects of the daily life of their resident family. This small group would know the comfort of consistent, unhurried care.

Elders would experience a comfortable approach to their day.

Step Five — Our dining services were hurried and dining rooms were crowded. Tables were cluttered with diet instructions. The noise levels were a disincentive to the enjoyment of meal time.

We would revamp entirely our approach to dining.

Step Six — Our physical plant was based on an outdated nursing home model. Long hallways cluttered with institutional equipment, limited amenity space, crowded dining rooms, and a nursing station that was the focal point with charts and equipment in clear view.

We would develop an architectural plan for renovation that would identify shortcomings and provide instead "home" for our elders.

Step Six — We had no resources for renovations, let alone staff re-education costs.

We would launch a capital campaign through The Christie Gardens Foundation to cover the cost of renovations and invest in staff selection and education.

Step Seven — No matter what investments we made, what capital renewal was planned, or what discussions and motivational meetings were held, the final outcome, whether successful or a failure, was dependent on the person who entered the elder's room and began to provide personal care.

We would develop an in-depth screening process and select the first neighbourhood team from our current staff.

Lesson Learned

"And let us not be weary in well doing: for in due season we shall reap, if we faint not" (Galatians 6:9, KJV). The key is to faint not!

En Route to Culture Change

The discussion with a resident, Mrs. Rose, followed my presentation to our independent living residents regarding our Culture Change initiative. The purpose of my meeting was not only to inform, but also to solicit financial support for the funds needed to create our first new neighbourhood. On behalf of The Christie Gardens Foundation, we were launching our million-dollar capital campaign.

I had met Mrs. Rose only once before and knew little of her history.

"Best wishes, Mrs. Sweatman. I admire your courage in attempting this initiative.

You do realize of course that culture change in an established organization will take 5 to 7 years. When I was hired by (a major US corporation) to establish a new manufacturing site, I was expected not only to see the plant operational but also to develop a new staffing model. It was a difficult challenge. I understand what lies ahead for you."

And here I thought she had been a secretary in the large corporation!

"We do hope to see it through in a much shorter time frame," I replied. She smiled kindly, promised a gift to the campaign, and left me to my own wishful thinking.

And now, six years later ...

I offer the following quote from Claudia, the director of education and advocacy at Christie Gardens. Claudia has been engaged actively in a leadership role since we began:

"It takes seven to ten years to fully own a culture change. Consistency and resolve are essential. Knowing exactly where you want to go, and having a very good idea of how to get there."

We are certainly older and wiser, but no less determined!

Now we are in our seventh year. I would like to believe we have achieved our Culture Change and will sustain it.

We had determined that our first neighbourhood, serving 24 elders, would be the pilot project for the remainder of The Courtyard community of 80 residents.

To achieve our goals, we encouraged all staff members to consider whether they would like to be part of this initiative. We would be posting positions for which they could apply. We advised them there would be a formal selection process, with in-depth training for the successful applicants.

The neighbourhood would be led by a new leader, a Neighbourhood Advocate.

A new model of service with newly created positions was very alarming to union representatives. They opposed our planned staff selection process, insisting on seniority as their only criteria for successful application. When we would not make this commitment, they actively counselled their members to not apply for the jobs we had posted.

Courage and curiosity won out over threats, with multiple applications for each post.

The screening process sought to determine whether the candidate could change their approach to care. To succeed, we would need to upset the established routines and practices that had been in place for many years, with which they were very comfortable. The process also looked at the attitude of the candidate toward the elders they were serving. It was very encouraging for the directors doing the interviews to have this reminder of the applicants' dedication.

Although the applicants began their interviews with uncertainty, they soon relaxed and responded well.

They exhibited an overall spirit of respect for and kindness toward the elders they served.

The selected team comprised both long-term employees, in some cases 25 years, as well as employees with much shorter tenure.

The union lodged grievances and launched arbitrations.

These were stress-inducing, time-consuming, and expensive. Our victories were no small relief. We were past the first major hurdle and would carry on.

Over time, respectful responses to union concerns, along with careful attention to our contracts, won out, and trust began to be restored.

Today a thoughtful mediation process with timely investigation of emerging issues has created a collaborative relationship between Christie Gardens and its unions.

There were certainly other areas where our optimism was sorely tested.

Our learning curve was very steep. We were often blindsided by unexpected outcomes. A new staffing model, new roles, and major redirections in leadership all required regular review and occasional tweaking.

We learned to respond carefully to murmurings. Not every predicted crisis would occur. Not every upset could be resolved. However, we did our best to never let dissent simmer.

Unrelenting determination, a clear vision, and a unified leadership team begin to win out over fear.

We would learn together. We would communicate, again and again.

We were successful in reaching the fundraising goal. However, with construction and permit challenges and resulting delays, our project took five years to complete. There are now three neighbourhoods, each with its own team. The outcomes are very satisfying, as is the level of demand for our service.

___

Lesson Learned

Vision "leaks" and must be reinforced again and again.

Culture Change Stories

L et me share some of the experiences from The Courtyard Community:

My friend, Miss Johnson, never had the opportunity to live in a newly renovated community. However, she did experience a fine quality of life satisfaction in her final years with us. She was able to relocate to a larger room, benefitted greatly from aggressive physiotherapy, and enjoyed effective personal care from a newly trained care partner. She will never know how her needs became the catalyst for the Culture Change.

You may remember the gentleman from the Call to Action whose admission was fraught with behavioural challenges and medication responses. He responded exceptionally well to his care partner and eventually the new environment. Medication prescribed to manage his behaviour was discontinued. Consistent, thoughtful attention was paid to his situation; he had been separated from his wife and was experiencing increased dementia.

In his final three years, mornings after breakfast were occupied with joining the group of gentlemen who regularly read the newspaper together. He became a welcoming face in the lounge and regaled others with good humour and storytelling. His restoration to a good quality of life in the midst of his dementia was a great comfort to me, and to his wife and children.

Miss Brown

Miss Brown was actively involved with her care partner in sorting and doing her own personal laundry. She expressed great satisfaction with the smell of freshly dried clothing and her ability to fold it the way she preferred before returning it to her room.

Mr. Lee

Mr. Lee loved to play his harmonica for his friends. He also offered pleasant comfort to his neighbours who were unable to participate in group activities, visiting in their rooms and performing for them.

Miss White

Miss White sat at the door of her room and chatted with those passing by. There was no sense of hurried or harried staff rushing through halls avoiding conversation because they were "too busy."

Miss Green

Miss Green had gradually become increasingly reclusive and difficult to serve. She barricaded her drawers and cupboards, fearing theft. She refused to join her neighbours in the dining room and would eat only if her meals were brought to her home. She became abrasive. Her hygiene deteriorated. She became physically resistant to care. No amount of health care intervention helped.

Mary, Miss Green's care partner, had a lengthy tenure with us as a personal support worker and had eagerly engaged in the in-depth training program in preparation for the new model of care. She was clearly ready to make the transition. Mary was one of the few staff members who Miss Green appeared to tolerate.

Mary had always expressed admiration and respect for elders — her training as a care partner reinforced those ideals and gave her a new appreciation for the importance of her role in the lives of her charges.

Fresh from her training and eager to apply the principles she had learned. Mary began an in-depth review of Miss Green's file. A fresh picture of Miss Green emerged. With newly acquired knowledge about her history, and the time available to spend with her, she carefully began conversations with Miss Green about her past, her teaching experiences, and about her sister.

Mary would chat while tidying Miss Green's room and making her bed. She would encourage Miss Green to assist her. She would gather the personal laundry and invite Miss Green to join her in the newly installed residents' laundry room. She encouraged her to participate in group events, and on the rare occasion when Miss Green agreed, Mary would accompany and introduce her. She offered to sit with Miss Green in the dining room when she was ready to join her neighbours for meals. She introduced her to the rest of her "family," her neighbours in The Courtyard.

Gradually, Mary experienced the joy of knowing her efforts were not in vain. Miss Green began to emerge from her reclusive hostile shell.

Within a few short weeks, the "buzz" of excited conversation began:

"Miss Green is coming to the dining room for all her meals."

"Miss Green let Mary unlock her cupboards."

"Miss Green invited other residents to join her at meals."

"Miss Green took the role of hostess at the dining room table."

"Miss Green visits new residents and welcomes them to her home."

"Miss Green invited her neighbours for tea."

Mary's posture toward Miss Green was born out of her respect for elders. She had been empowered, given a realistic workload, and received support and encouragement to become acquainted and build a relationship with Miss Green.

Mary engaged Miss Green in the care of her room and belongings. She encouraged her to set her own pace in her daily activities. She identified and encouraged Miss Green's capacity for hospitality. She accompanied her to the dining room at the time chosen by Miss Green, and assisted her in the role of resident hostess.

Miss Green spent another two years "at home at Christie Gardens." She was a pleasure to serve. Her final days were punctuated by visits from residents and the staff team who knew and cared for her. She became an example that gave affirmation to our oft-stated conviction: "There is a better way."

These observations of individual successes occurred early in our journey. The overall success continues to this day.

The dining room has become an especially attractive place to be. Our elders experience the sight and sound of food preparation with dining services staff members who engage in conversation with those who arrive early. There were no labels or diet directives on the tables to constantly remind them of their health status.

The hours of service in the dining room have been expanded. The rush to meal time with elders lined up waiting to enter a closed dining room is a thing of the past. The care partners escort them to their seat when they arrive. If they're early, they're greeted with the offer of a beverage until their table mates join them.

Each care partner responds to her group of elders with their individual wishes. Where care needs of an elder might increase for a time, the care partners rally to assist each other. Each neighbourhood is its own vibrant community, not just a hallway of private rooms.

There is no medication cart in the dining room. Nurses can visit them in their rooms. This approach provides opportunity for feedback from the elder or their care partner, in their private space, at home.

Breakfast time is very relaxed. Some of the gentlemen enjoy their morning coffee at the raised counter in front of the kitchen. The kitchen is open throughout the day. Families are encouraged to share a meal or a break time with the elder they're visiting.

As can sometimes occur with elders experiencing dementia, disruptive and ongoing calling-out might occur. The team is dedicated to collaborating together to understand and address the underlying cause rather than attempting to suppress the behaviour by whatever means.

Care partners and their neighbourhood advocate reach out to the nurse to join them in the discussion. Together they consider possible solutions. They are empowered to implement them, with frequent review and ongoing discussion. This shared activity has been very effective and satisfying for all concerned.

Supporting the efforts of the care partners are the steady hands of the neighbourhood advocates.

The role of neighbourhood advocate has proven pivotal in the success of the neighbourhoods. Each advocate does just that — she advocates for the elders, their care partners, and all else who need her attention. Each member of this unique team supports their colleagues in managing the challenges of every day. They in turn collaborate regularly with their leader, the director of education and advocacy.

In the midst of our satisfaction with the outcomes of the Culture Change, we never lose sight of the frailty and complex needs of those we serve. The atmosphere continues to be respectful and kind to the elders and to those empowered to serve them.

Lesson Learned:

There was indeed a better way!

There Was a Better Way

We are privileged to serve the elders who join our family. We are determined to serve with excellence. We seek actively to understand what matters most to the elders we serve. We are relentless in our pursuit of "the better way" in our ever-changing world.

**I am trusting we will influence others
to seek their own "better way."**

I continue to be motivated by Micah 6:8: "As much as we can, we will do justly, love mercy, and walk humbly."

Afterword

A Family Affair

I had the great good fortune of experiencing and benefitting from the dedicated, highly skilled, and invaluable commitment of members of my family.

I remember well my first foray into family engagement. My children had been listening to my stories for several years. They knew I loved both them and the seniors I served. It felt like a family affair.

Fellowship Towers needed full-time security services. The daytime shift was a simple matter, with candidates readily available.

Not so the weekends and evenings.

These were difficult shifts to fill, with frequent turnover and lack of commitment on the part of the young staff members selected for this role.

My three sons were in their late teens and early twenties. They were experienced in work and valued the income. Our home had been a depot for newspapers and advertising flyers for delivery. They had been babysitters, had shovelled snow for neighbours, and in one notable experience, my eldest son had managed the student schedules for his high school, and been paid to do so. They were all still in school.

They knew that mother would be a demanding taskmaster and that only good news should come out of their work.

And so the Sweatman boys and a few of their friends became the security team on evenings, weekends, and holidays.

They replaced each other when shift changes were needed. They were dependable and respectful to those who served and were served. They observed a strict dress code. They carried pagers and never left a shift uncovered.

My middle son expressed it well. "Being a PK, 'Preacher's Kid,' might be tough, but being a BK, 'Boss's Kid,' was tougher". Mom was a determined taskmaster, but we loved the work and served well between us for several years. We still have memories of key personalities and exciting experiences. The evolution into full-time careers in the field of serving our elders for several of us was a natural one."

In time, the three boys and their younger sister all worked at Christie Gardens. Today, of the five children and their five spouses, seven of them work full-time in various leadership roles and in several seniors communities. The communities are enriched by their dependable and gifted commitment.

And the legacy continues.

After many years in various posts at Christie Gardens and elsewhere, my youngest daughter succeeded me as CEO at Christie Gardens. She is thriving in the role, as is Christie Gardens. She has recently completed the very demanding EMBA program.

My eldest son, having worked as a business owner in the manufacturing sector for many years, is now the successful executive director of a sister home and serves Christie Gardens as its extremely capable CFO. His experience in business has been invaluable.

My middle son is skilled in construction project management, having served faithfully and well as Project Manager during the addition of the life lease suites at Christie Gardens. He continues in project management, including ongoing apartment renovations. He also manages their family business, that of an agency providing top quality private duty and replacement staff in the field of health care.

My youngest son provides IT support 24/7 through his company. He's responsible for all communications and social media. The evidence of his skill is in the excellent branding and public presentation of Christie Gardens. He will not compromise in the quality of printed materials. He's also the editor of this collection of stories about my experiences in eldercare. This publication would not have been possible without him.

My eldest daughter graduated with a degree in Psychology and English, culminating with her honours thesis on successful aging. She married a scientist in the field of health care technology. They live in another city, but continue to contribute in this important, growing area

These children all have a very keen sense of ownership of this not-for-profit community. They share the values and respect for the elders. They understand the challenges of selecting and training qualified staff teams. Several of their children are exploring career options in this field as well.

At the time of this recollection of experiences, three of my grandsons, all university students, now fulfill the same roles as their fathers had experienced — security staff members, evenings and weekends!

Once again, these are difficult roles to fill. Christie Gardens residents speak to me often of their pleasure in talking with these fine young men.

And if there were other ones with suitable skills, I would not let the last name deter me from seeking their participation in the adventure of eldercare.

Thank you, family. I love you.

And finally, thank you, dear reader, for joining me on my Joyful Journey. My dream is that you will be encouraged by the lessons learned, in whatever field of endeavour you enjoy.

My vision is that those serving elders might be challenged to consider The Better Way.

My gratitude is extended to The Christie Gardens Foundation, without whose support this memoir would not have been possible.

Onward!